VGM Careers for

D0439091

CAREERS FOR

SPORTS
NUTS

& Other Athletic Types

RAY HEITZMANN

THIRD EDITION

VGM Career Books

Chicago   New York   San Francisco   Lisbon   London   Madrid   Mexico City
Milan   New Delhi   San Juan   Seoul   Singapore   Sydney   Toronto

The McGraw·Hill Companies

Library of Congress Cataloging-in-Publication Data

Heitzmann, Ray
 Careers for sports nuts & other athletic types / By Ray Heitzmann — 3rd ed.
  p. cm. — (VGM careers for you series)
  ISBN 0-07-141158-5
  1. Sports—Vocational guidance. I. Title: Careers for sports nuts and
 other athletic types. II. Title. III. Series.

 GV734.3.H445 2004
 796'.024—dc22   2003025812

2 3 4 5 6 7 8 9 0   LBM/LBM   3 2 1 0 9 8 7 6 5 4

ISBN 0-07-141158-5

McGraw-Hill books are available at special quantity discounts to use as premiums and sales promotions, or for use in corporate training programs. For more information, please write to the Director of Special Sales, Professional Publishing, McGraw-Hill, Two Penn Plaza, New York, NY 10121-2298. Or contact your local bookstore.

This book is printed on acid-free paper.

Contents

Foreword

I shall never forget that fall evening in 1972. I was a sophomore attending Springfield Southeast High in my hometown of Springfield, Illinois—the heart of what we considered to be the most fertile prep basketball cropland in America.

I was a player. I was not a great player, but I was on the roster. During those days, that alone was a sufficient magnet to capture the occasional coed's attention.

The problem was, I wanted to be a great player in the worst of ways. What a thrill it would be to play above the rim in Fighting Illini blue and orange as the crowd howled its approval. "Air Fred" shoes seemed a natural. Perhaps an MVP award or two along the way.

These were but some of the daydreams I was entertaining there at the far end of the bench when, for the first time in my basketball career, I was summoned by the coach to enter a contest. At first, I thought it to be a rather cruel joke. After all, mine was the only uniform in SSHS history to have never required laundering. Why waste soap on something that wasn't soiled?

The reality of the situation finally seeped in. The warrior was being called to arms. I sprinted onto the floor, not realizing things such as removal of warm-ups and checking in with the scorer needed to be done first. These trivial impediments to my mission attended to, I hit the floor with a vengeance, wanting one thing and one thing only—I wanted to score. This was my chance. Perhaps my only chance. The entire Western world knew that the only way for a JV player to get his name into the box score of the local paper was by scoring points. Fouls, assists, rebounds . . . none of those counted. Only the deuce.

Three quick fouls; each might have been punishable by five to ten in the state pen had they been committed on the street.

Then, the jump ball. The tip went to my best friend, Leo Thompson. I flew out on the wing, crying, begging, pleading for the ball. Leo, swayed by the siren-sound of my calls, passed me the object of my desire and I put in one of the prettiest finger-roll lay-ups you've ever seen.

But, why was there no cheering? Where was the adulation? This was my home court, and yet not one soul seemed to appreciate my effort.

For a moment, I thought I might have lost my hearing. That's when I saw that face, that nameless face in the second row. The one with what seemed to be two sets of teeth. The one crying . . . with laughter.

Fred Hickman, "Air Fred," had soared to and scored at the other team's basket.

It became clear to me at that moment in my life that I would never be a professional athlete. But, my dear love of sports continued to grow at a fever pace. The only outlet I could find was sportscasting, and what a treasure it's been. Kind of like taking a trip without leaving the farm.

I have covered the big deals. The World Series. The Super Bowl. The NBA Finals. But I've also been blessed with seeing those magical midseason moments that are forgotten by those who were not there. Don Kessinger's inside-the-parker against the Pirates at Wrigley. Jim McMahon bringing the Bears back to beat the Vikings that Monday night.

The men and women I've met and the friendships I've made in this business are worth twice their weight in gold: Julius Erving, Satchell Paige, Gordie Howe, Michael Jordan. The list alone would make the casual fan green with envy and could easily fill several chapters of this work. My life has been enriched in countless ways through my career in sports journalism. It has provided me with the vehicle to earn a better than decent living for my wife, Judith, and our family. It has allowed me to bring the fan the games through my eyes. Sports has allowed me to be a positive role model for other aspiring young black sports journalists, which is a tremendous honor.

Besides, nobody's had the guts to mention my scoring for the wrong team in years—an added plus. And, imagine, I've never once had to go on injured reserve or hold out or be traded for a sportscaster to be named later.

Yes, I enjoy the best of both worlds in this business of sports. Many others in different disciplines related to sports will tell you the same thing in the following pages.

Bet you never imagined the wide, wide world of sports could be this wide!

Fred Hickman
CNN Sports

Acknowledgments

The author would like to thank the many players, coaches, and associated people who have contributed to his love and knowledge of sports. In terms of this book, the author wishes to thank the following:

Regina Agrusa
Julie K. Anthony
Dan Baker
Ronnie Barnes, M.S., ATC
Ed Barycki
Mary Beilinske
Jack Bell
Jose Bernal
Richard Borkowski, Ed.D.
Bill Brousseau
Bill Buckner
Don Casey
Kenneth Clarke, Ph.D.
Andrew Clary
Martin Clein, M.D.
James Clinkingbeard
Lee Cohen, DPM
George Colfer
Michael Colgan
Terry Conway
Jim Corea, Ph.D., RPT
Jerry Crawford

Joe Crawford
Stephanie Cugini
Karen Hargadon Daly
Vic D'Ascenzo
Donald Davidson
Otho Davis
Jim Delorenzo
Donna de Varonna
Craig Dimitri
Vincent DiStefano, M.D.
Mike DiTrolio
Mary Edgerly
Page Elliott
William Emper, M.D.
Ronald Feingold, Ph.D.
Ric Flair
Ann Fisher
Burt Fisher, M.D.
Theodore Fox, M.D.
Vincent Francia
Stephanie Gaitley
Bill Gallo

Stan Gallup
Frances Garmon
Rose Gatti
Jerry Gay
Eric Germunder
Joel Goodhart
Clara Gordon
Howard "Dr. Bucky" Grace
Ann Grandsean, Ph.D.
Dick Hall
Mike Hall
Larry Hanzel
R. C. Haygood, Ph.D.
Pat Harmon
Tom Harmon
Steve Hebb
Hank Iervolino
Keith Jackson
King Kaluha
Gerry Kaplan
Richard Kaufman, M.D.
Dean Kenefick
I. Lawrence Kerr, D.D.S.
Ed Kershner
Earl "Skip" Kingwill
Kerry Kittles
Barbara Kratchman
Kimberly Kumiega
David Lamb
Bob Lambert
Tony Leodora
Cathy Leonard
Janet Lippincott
Victor Livingston
Susan M. London

Jackie Lopin
John Lumber
Eddie Malloy
Barry Mano
Larry Mathews, Ed.D.
Philip J. Mayer, M.D.
Tim McCarver
Mike McClain
Mike McDyre
Andy McGovern
James McHugh
Joe McIlvanie
Peggy Kerschner McKernan
Dave Meggyesy
Bernard Meltzer
Ed Miersch, M.A., ATC
E. Don Miller
Henry Miller, M.D.
Craig Morgan, M.D.
Heide Lee Morgan
Mike Moriarity
Carl Morris, Ph.D.
Dave Morway
Pat Mosher, Ph.D.
Anne Moss
Andrew Myers, B.S., CPO
Dave Neiskens
Vince Nicastro
Henry Nichols, Ed.D.
Stacie Nichols
Michael O'Shea
Violet Palmer
Shelley Pennefather
Richie Phillips
Millie Puccio

Ted Quedenfeld

Henry Reiter, Ph.D.

John Robinson

Jim Rohr

Gil Roman

Edward Rose

Sam Rosenthal

Bob Rotella

Ed Sabol

Michael Sachs

Gale Sayers

Larry Schoppet

Betsy Scott

Larry Shane

Michele Sharp

Deena Shelton

Neal Sherman

Sarah Short, Ph.D.

Paul Smith

Richard M. Swinn, Ph.D.

Andy Talley

Lynn Tighe

Dan Unger, ATC

Ron Valmassy, D.P.M.

Julie Victor

Marty Walsh

D. Weight

Helen Welde

Harry Wendelstedt

Tim Whitaker

Jill White, Ph.D.

Kenny Williams

Rick Wolff

Derek Wright

Jay Wright

Jerold Zebrick

Sincere thanks to Rick and Mary Heitzmann for their support, as well as to Villanova University and to the Ragdale Foundation, Lake Forest, Illinois, for their support during the preparation of the original manuscript. Thanks also goes to Mark Rowh, the talented and resourceful writer who assisted with the second edition.

A dedication is made to four basketball players I had the privilege to coach who have passed—Mike Dudick, North Chicago High School (Illinois); Teddy Fikes, Highland Falls High School (New York); Ken Golder, Villanova University NiteCats (Pennsylvania); and Brendon Kelly, Neumann College (Pennsylvania).

In addition to my family and the family of sports enthusiasts everywhere, a special thank you is made to Peggy Moses Melnick, Kathleen Esnes Heitzmann, and G. Linda Criscuolo.

Introduction

People love sports. From the great tradition of Canadian hockey to the excitement of baseball during spring training in Florida, people of all ages and backgrounds make sports a part of their lives—both as an avocation and as a vocation.

Today, sports is show business. In many ways it's the fusing of business (often big business) and entertainment—Hollywood style. This sports phenomenon, which has become a religion for some and an obsession for others, may have a career for you. The jobs stretch from the coaches who shape athletic talent to the publicists who promote it.

An amazingly high level of job satisfaction categorizes this area, from the sports equipment salesperson selling bats and bowling balls to the agent insuring players and playing fields. June Hannah, wife of successful college baseball coach, Bob Hannah (supersuccessful University of Delaware baseball coach—recently retired), nicely summarized the situation: "I don't mind the number of hours Bob spends with baseball. I'm just glad he is so happy with his career when so many people dislike their jobs."

The profession is likewise characterized by long hours of hard work and dedication. Bob Terry, retired championship wrestling coach at North Chicago High School, described one point during his coaching career: "I was working so many hours that I probably averaged a salary of twenty-five cents per hour!"

Outsiders often see only the glamour of sports careers—the limelight, big bucks, glory, and recognition. For every star who is a household name, there are a hundred laboring in the shadows.

Even so, these unknowns (or locally knowns) love what they are doing.

This book should be read in its entirety. It explains the great interdependence among careers. For example, the successful football coach relies upon the ground crew, the sports information publicist, the statistician, the athletic trainer, and others. The successful minor league baseball team general manager relies upon the director of concessions, the marketing/sales manager, the sportswriters, the radio broadcasters, and the team manager, among others. You will obtain an appreciation of these interrelations through a complete reading of the work.

The quickest route to obtaining a position in the field involves meshing an existing skill or specialty with sports. A lawyer could refocus toward becoming a sports agent. A nurse may take additional course work in athletic training to enter the profession. A computer specialist may wish to run the centerfield scoreboard, including "Fanavision," or tabulate sports statistics to discover trends and patterns. A dental technician might switch jobs to work with a dentist who caters to a sports clientele. A landscaper could design baseball diamonds. A radio announcer may specialize in broadcasting professional wrestling. An accountant might serve as a business manager for a college athletic department. Similarly, photographers, computer specialists, writers, and others can redirect their energies (sometimes with additional education) toward a self-fulfilling—and occasionally a lucrative—life in sports.

One ingredient remains a must for all sports careers: interpersonal skills. Sports is a people business. You absolutely must be able to work with people, often under stress—losing streaks, deadlines, negotiations, game injuries, and budget inadequacies.

The ability to bring to sports the experience and knowledge from another profession (or obtain the same through schooling) and couple it with people skills, a sense of humor, and a high energy level will result in a winning career. This refers not only to Max Plotkin, Crazy George, Donkey Basketball, the Harlem

Globetrotters, Streetball, Daredevils Slam Dunk Show, and the Chicken, but everyone!

The author hopes that this book will enhance your understanding of the vast domain of sports careers and will assist you in entering that life, resulting in personal and professional success while contributing to a better world of sports.

CHAPTER ONE

Athletic Coaches

Some athletic coaches earn salaries in the millions of dollars. Some coaches win championships. Some achieve fame on television and related media. However, most athletic coaches work to assist their players to achieve athletic and academic success as well as success in life. These coaches achieve their success at middle and high schools; small colleges; summer recreation programs; church-, temple-, and synagogue-sponsored activities; and related situations. While there may be no limelight, these jobs involve major commitment and stress—as well as major rewards.

Professional Coaching

The prestige and salaries of professional coaches command everyone's attention. However, when their teams lose regularly, coaches quickly become the victims of fans on radio sports talk shows and print and electronic media commentators. Yet many love it and stay in the profession, despite poor job security, and even return after dismissal. This author has often theorized that the great highs and lows of the job at all levels must make it addictive.

The career of Don Casey, former head coach of the National Basketball Association's Los Angeles Clippers and New Jersey Nets, is typical of many who have achieved success at this lofty level. Coach Casey paid his dues at the high school level, culminating in his team, Bishop Eustace High School, winning the New Jersey state championship. He broke the record as the youngest coach to win the New Jersey championship when he was just twenty-two.

Coach Casey joined the basketball staff at Temple University following his tenure as a high school coach. First serving as an assistant coach and later as head coach, he continued to experience success. Prior to his service with the Clippers, he coached in Italy, at Notre Dame University, and as an assistant with the Chicago Bulls. Clearly, the road to professional coaching is characterized by a difficult journey, but if you love your sport and love coaching, you won't feel the bumps along the road as much.

Lifestyles and Preparation

Most professional coaches have played the game they coach—many at the professional level. Depending on their visibility and popularity, some start their coaching careers as assistant coaches at the college or professional level. With success, they move to head coach status. Unfortunately, some move too quickly from player to head coach and amass a number of losses, quickly joining the ranks of the unemployed.

In addition to an intimate knowledge of the sport and extensive experience with it, professional-level head coaches need expert skills in dealing with players, the media, and fans. Likewise, they must motivate very well-paid athletes to play hard and to continue to improve their skills. Often, head coaches have expert organizational skills as they juggle their exceptionally busy schedules, involving everything from luncheon presentations and talk show interviews to reviewing videotapes of previous games and evaluation of potential draft picks.

Assistant coaches' duties at this level vary greatly. Normally, they have a special expertise: for example, defensive end coach, strength and training coach, or pitching coach. Teams frequently have a number of specialists who work with the team in a consulting capacity: nutritionist, sports psychologist, exercise physiologist, and others.

Considerable hoopla surrounds professional sports teams, and no one can discount the glamour, the prestige, or the satisfaction of earned success. As with others in professional sports, coaches' salaries have escalated greatly, with head coaches of major sports often earning more than a million dollars a year and assistant coaches exceeding several hundred thousand. Media attention focuses no brighter anywhere in America than on winning professional coaches, nor does so little sympathy exist for a deposed loser. Fortunately, many of the skills necessary in coaching, such as organizational ability and skill in working with people, are useful in the business world. Consequently, most former pro coaches find employment in sales, public relations, and management. Others return to teaching while retaining an involvement in sports by serving part-time as scouts. A fortunate few find careers as sports announcers.

The interest in sports shows no signs of slowing. There will be a continuing need for the few who make it to the select group designated as "professional coaches."

School Coaching

Assistant Coach

The explosion of boys' and girls' sports in elementary, middle or junior high, and senior high schools has created extensive opportunities for potential coaches. Many school athletic directors aggressively seek men and women to coach sports ranging from middle school girls' field hockey and softball to high school boys' wrestling and football. They may even be forced to hire novices with little knowledge of the sport or of young people! The term *assistant coach* is used here to refer to all school coaches except the varsity head coach at the high school.

The ability to work with young people ranks as a major priority in selection of personnel. Intelligence and common sense plus some knowledge of the following will prove beneficial: first aid, legal issues related to coaching, practice organization, conditioning, motor skill development relative to the sport in question, coaching strategy, motivational techniques, and bench coaching.

Additional knowledge in areas such as strength and fitness development, nutrition, or current developments in training and conditioning will aid any coach.

If you coach in a cross-gender situation, for example, as a male coaching a women's team, you will need additional preparation. *Go Girl: Raising Healthy, Confident, and Successful Girls Through Sports* (Sourcebooks Trade), a recent book by Hannah Storm, can help you to prepare because, as the author states, "women are good for the game because they play the same game, but do it differently than men . . . female athletes bring a fresh perspective to the game." The sports industry agrees that the explosion of women in athletics at all levels has been very, very positive.

Do school coaches need to serve as physical educators or teachers in the schools at which they coach? At one time this was true, but not today. Many schools utilize part-time coaches at all levels. These individuals have full-time jobs that permit them to coach practice in the late afternoon and participate in games on weekday afternoons and weekends. Usually these coaches love their sport and working with young people. They often attend workshops, clinics, and summer and off-season camps, as well as read and study games extensively to improve their skills and move to the next level.

Some school districts have excellent traditions of success in some sports and have dominated their regions and states. School administrators and the community carefully select and monitor even assistant coaches in their favored sports. Fierce competition for these positions exists, and the salaries tend to be higher than those of other sports. Typically, annual assistant coaching salaries range from $500 to $5,000. For instance, a middle school basketball coach may earn $1,200 and an assistant for varsity football may earn $3,000.

Often it's the assistant coach who makes a major contribution to the development of young people, as players develop their love of a sport and build work habits and fundamental skills at the prevarsity level. While a varsity coach may receive adulation or criticism for the team's performance, it's often the junior varsity coach who has made the difference.

Most coaches aspire to become a head coach. Following a successful apprenticeship as an assistant, they may move to the top position.

Head Coach

Rarely does the public know of the amount and variety of tasks performed by head coaches. A partial list of these activities follows:

- conducting postseason evaluations of the players, assistant coaches, and oneself, which normally involves several meetings and conferences
- taking inventory and ordering new equipment
- discussing scheduling with the athletic director and opposing coaches
- arranging for preseason scrimmage games
- recruiting team managers and statisticians
- meeting regularly with assistant coaches
- attending preseason workshops, clinics, and conferences for coaches
- making a schedule for scouting opponents
- announcing tryouts
- writing press releases for newspapers
- planning for use of athletic facilities
- clipping newspaper stories on the team and its opponents
- inviting the players' parents to the games
- monitoring players' academic progress
- asking knowledgeable persons to scout the team for weaknesses
- arranging videotaping of the team
- analyzing videotapes for strategy
- encouraging players to attend summer sports camp and participate in summer sports

- assisting players in their choice of colleges
- discussing the program and problems with the school principal and other administrators
- writing thank-you letters to appropriate individuals

If the above list looks like difficult work, you are correct; coaching is not easy. At the school level, few enter for financial reasons. Perhaps the numerous required duties lead many coaches to early retirement. It should be remembered that most coaches have regular teaching duties to properly execute (such as class preparation, test correction, and course planning) as their primary obligation.

Because of turnover within coaching and the expansion of sports, many opportunities exist for coaching employment. Salaries vary with the emphasis the community places upon the sport, as well as local wage and salary practices. For example, a school district that regards football as very important may pay a coach $10,000 a season, while another district may pay $3,000. Coaches of minor sports—tennis, wrestling, and swimming— may receive less than $1,000, unless there is strong local interest. Naturally, this is in addition to a teaching salary.

Also, many coaches at all levels in all sports direct summer camps or assist in such activities. This can be a welcome source of extra income.

At the school level, coaching, which is really an avocation, offers the opportunity to work closely with a group of young people and have a large impact upon their development. Many of the friendships made will be carried throughout the coach's life and provide a continuing source of satisfaction.

Most coaches make a positive difference!

College Coaching

College coaching varies greatly with the visibility of the program and the status of the college or university. That is, a Division I (or

IAA for football) NCAA program at a major university undoubtedly has significant coverage of its games by the media and often has its games televised. This is not true of Division II, III, or NAIA programs, although the latter receives regular newspaper and periodic television coverage. So, if you wish to be a superstar college coach on the television, aspire to Division I status. It's well to remember that many coaches greatly enjoy the small colleges and often achieve tenure there, far from the limelight.

Michele Sharp knew in high school that she wanted to coach basketball and perhaps some other sports. While enrolled at West Chester University in the health and physical education program, she served as an assistant coach in basketball and softball at nearby Cabrini College. Upon graduation, she gained employment as a health and physical education teacher and as head coach in softball and basketball. Sharp remained active in the off-season through coaching Amateur Athletic Union (AAU) teams and working at summer basketball camps. Following successful stops at Philadelphia College of Textile and Science, Swarthmore College, and Norwich University, she now coaches at Manhattan College in Riverdale, New York.

"I love the players and enjoy the camaraderie of the coaches, and winning makes the hard work all worth it," she said, adding that she believes that "opportunities for women in coaching abound. Although we don't have the extensive professional system men do, jobs are now available for women coaching men."

Volunteer Coaching

The opportunity of having a positive effect on young people is probably available in coaching more than in any other sports career. Nowhere is this truer than among volunteer coaches. Thousands of these coaches at all levels labor daily to develop their players to win games or events. The profession can be very rewarding, challenging, and fulfilling; but many days are hectic, tiring, and, unfortunately, thankless. Recently some coaches have openly expressed their disappointment in the lack of dedication of some athletes; that is, players who have sidetracked themselves—playing video games or hanging out—instead of committing themselves to self-improvement. Fortunately, the majority of athletes are more dedicated.

THE BILL OF RIGHTS FOR YOUNG ATHLETES

No one should coach unless he or she is familiar with and can implement "The Bill of Rights for Young Athletes." It serves as an excellent guideline for youth program coaches. Many of these rights should also be observed by coaches of high school and older players.

1. Right to have the opportunity to participate in sports regardless of ability level.
2. Right to participate at a level that is commensurate with each child's development level.
3. Right to have qualified adult leadership.
4. Right to participate in safe, healthy environments.
5. Right of each child to share in the leadership and decision making of their sport participation.
6. Right to play as a child and not as an adult.
7. Right to proper preparation for participation in the sport.
8. Right to equal opportunity to strive for success.
9. Right to be treated with dignity by all involved.
10. Right to have fun through sport.

Many part-time and some full-time coaching situations exist for the interested volunteer; it's a wonderful entry into the profession. For those with a knowledge of their sport, an appreciation of children and young adults, and a desire to work daily to improve themselves, opportunities abound.

Most neighborhood, church, and community teams rely heavily upon volunteers to coach teams of young people. Little League Baseball, Police Athletic League (PAL), Pop Warner Football, Young Men's Christian Association (YMCA), Young Men's Hebrew Association (YMHA), Young Women's Christian Association (YWCA), Catholic Youth Organization (CYO), Optimist Youth Athletic programs, American Legion Baseball, youth soccer leagues, and many similar groups could not serve the millions of players they do without the free services of volunteer coaches. While some receive a salary, usually it is very little when the amount of time is considered. Yet, while the income may be none or little, the responsibility remains great—most often it is here that children receive their first experience with organized sports.

In recent years, it has become fashionable to criticize the abuses and mistakes of volunteer coaches. While some of this is clearly justified—a few coaches have overemphasized winning and underemphasized development of players and have poor practice organization—the vast majority of volunteer coaches make a substantial contribution.

Acting as a volunteer coach can serve as an enjoyable outlet while you help others. Unfortunately, many people take on the job with little information about the role and only superficial knowledge of the sport. In some cases, awkward situations and legal problems have occurred because of an injury or improper handling of behavior problems.

It is extremely important for any coach working with youngsters to prepare for the assignment. Experienced coaches realize that youngsters notice how a coach dresses and talks, handles emotion, uses fair standards, and knows the rules of the sport. They also understand that coaches may be held liable for any physical harm incurred by players in their charge.

Coaching is basically teaching, and good coaches build not only good athletes but also good citizens. Regina Agrusa, girl's lacrosse coach at Elmont High School on Long Island, New York, embodies these ideas. "I love athletic coaching because through it I can help to empower young girls," said Agrusa. "The athletic field is a place where life skills can be taught. I aid my players to be confident and feel good about themselves as they work individually and together for success." Coach Agrusa serves as director of guidance and counseling services at the Elmont High School; she has been named coach of the year and served as a championship coach on Long Island.

Preparing to Coach

If you're planning a career as a coach, the time to begin is now. The following abilities have been listed by the American Alliance for Health, Physical Education, Recreation, and Dance as necessary for the prospective coach. In preparing for your career, try to develop the following qualities:

- an understanding of the relationship of the interscholastic program and the particular sport you are coaching to the total education program
- a knowledge of first aid and the safety practices and techniques pertinent to the sport you are coaching
- an understanding of the possibilities of legal liability as well as sound safety practices and preventive measures
- a thorough knowledge and understanding of the biological, social, moral, emotional, and spiritual values that may accrue from the activity and the best methods of bringing about these desirable outcomes
- a knowledge of the most acceptable principles of growth and development and their implications for the sport
- an understanding of the basic principles in the care and prevention of injuries, together with an understanding of the proper relationship of the coach to the school or team physician
- an understanding of the best methods of developing and conditioning members of athletic squads

- the ability to speak in public to bring credit to the profession and the school and to more effectively inform the public of the educational possibilities of the sport
- an understanding of the basic psychological principles of motivation, stress, play, and group interaction
- a thorough knowledge of the fundamentals, offenses, defenses, strategies, and teaching methods involved in a particular sport (including squad organization, coaching techniques, and sound motivational procedures)
- a knowledge and sense of responsibility for local, state, and national rules

If you go to college to become a physical education teacher, you should achieve all of the above. People who either don't attend college or declare another major will need to prepare themselves.

All those wishing to enter the ranks of one of the most valuable, most important, and most fun professions should consider the following additional suggestions:

1. Begin reading and developing a library of books, articles, and clippings on coaching the sport of your interest. For example, a track coach should regularly read *Track Coach*, a quarterly journal covering techniques of this sport. Other publications worth reviewing include *Scholastic Coach and Athletic Director*, *Soccer Journal*, *Track and Field Coaches Review*, and *Canadian Journal for Health, Physical Education, Recreation, and Dance*. A number of fine videos also exist on both specific (Mike Fratello, *Three-Point Strategy*) and general (Lou Holtz, *Changing Adversity into Opportunity*) topics. A very good basic book for all coaches is *Successful Coaching* by Rainer Martens (Leisure Press), National Federation Interscholastic Coaches Education Program Edition. It provides information on everything from developing a coaching philosophy to nutrition for athletes. Likewise, another good book for

both coaches and players is *Faith in Sports* (Doubleday). The following websites are also helpful: www.geenatakes aim.com on young women in athletics; www.thecoaching store.com, providing "information plus" to youth league coaches; and www.strongerathlete.com for your players.

2. Attend practices of several teams at various levels to observe other coaches' organization and teaching techniques. This is important not only for nonathletes, but also for those who have participated in sports. It's easy to fall into the trap of coaching the way you were coached. Take the best and incorporate it into your system.

3. Observe as many games, matches, or meets as you can. While doing so, become a student of the sport. Observe how a coach performs magic or makes a mistake. For example, in basketball, how does the coach use time-outs? In hockey, how are substitutions handled? In football, what adjustments are made at halftime? In softball, exactly when is a relief pitcher brought in to replace the starter? Quite often, the difference between a fan and a person actually studying a game is that the fan watches only the main action (usually the ball), while the keen observer also watches the behavior of the other players and the actions of the coach's individual assistants.

4. Study and memorize the rules and rule changes of your sport so that, as coach, you will be knowledgeable in using the rules for your benefit and that of your team. Strategy frequently revolves around the rules of the game, with coaches working to gain an advantage. State athletic associations (governing bodies) provide rule booklets. You may also wish to obtain an NCAA read easy rules booklet. For more information, contact the National Collegiate Athletic Association, listed at the end of this chapter.

5. Select some coaches whom you admire and use them as role models for yourself. You may want to write and ask them to share some of their materials with you. Many

coaches will provide information on their approaches to the sport, including specifics in areas such as practice organization and weight training. A coaching model need not have a fantastic record; many coaches are very good yet have only mediocre win-loss histories.

6. Discover what functions sports officials, scorekeepers, statisticians, and athletic directors perform at an athletic event. If you do not have athletic ability, you may wish to volunteer to serve as a manager or statistician for a team. One of the best ways to gain an excellent close-up feel for athletics is to serve as a referee, judge, or umpire. Not only does this enable you to practice instant recall of the rules, but you also gain an insight into the flow of the event. Frequently, lower-level sports teams go begging for officials. Volunteer—it will make you a better coach.

7. Investigate the off-season techniques to develop players in your sport. For example, weight training equipment and procedures, conditioning, and nutrition have changed dramatically in recent years. Future coaches should stay informed about these developments. Observe athletes and their coaches in working situations during the off-season.

8. Attend professional meetings, conferences, and clinics, and join the coaching associations related to your sports interest. Membership in the professional organizations listed at the end of this chapter is strongly encouraged.

9. Participate in sports. If you are unable to compete at the varsity level, play on intramural and community teams.

10. Volunteer to serve as an assistant coach for a team of children in your community. This will give you the experience as well as the opportunity to learn and experiment in developing your own coaching system and philosophy.

Coaching can be one of the most positive and wholesome careers our society has to offer. In order to realize the many benefits, a tremendous commitment of time and energy is needed—and the earlier you begin, the better. If you think it may not be worth it, consider the following excerpt from an article titled "Thoughts About My Coach," from the magazine *Young Athlete.*

•••••••••••••••••••••••••••••

"Back in the early 1920s, when I was in the seventh grade at West Orange, New Jersey's, Fairmount Middle School, I met a man who changed my whole life. His name was Lawrence Quallo, our athletic director. . . . As a youngster I was not a very good athlete, but I did my best. Then one day on the basketball court, after I had been lucky enough to score, Mr. Quallo stopped the game, came over to me and asked, 'Eddie, would you like to try out for our team? . . . I think you have the makings of a good player.'

"Thanks to Larry Quallo's influence, I went on to become a fairly good three-letter man in high school. So much did Larry inspire and guide me that, when I was in my junior year of high school, I scored over one thousand points for the basketball team (missed only one foul shot), scored eleven touchdowns, and ran the hundred in ten seconds flat. I tried to please Larry. My reward? He said he was more than pleased. That was enough. . . .

"I'm now in the Hall of Fame, but only because of Larry. He helped my dreams come true. He put a real foundation under my dreams, insuring they'd become reality. He was like a father to me, and I bless his memory every day of my life."

•••

For More Information

Coaching Association of Canada
141 Laurier Avenue West, Suite 300
Ottawa, ON K1P 5J3
Canada
www.coach.ca

National Alliance for Youth Sports
2050 Vista Parkway
West Palm Beach, FL 33411
www.nays.org

National Association of Basketball Coaches
9300 West 110th Street, Suite 640
Overland Park, KS 66210
www.nabc.com

National Collegiate Athletic Association
700 West Washington Street
P.O. Box 6222
Indianapolis, IN 46206
www.ncaa.org

National High School Athletic Coaches Association
P.O. Box 4342
Hamden, CT 06514
www.hscoaches.org

National Youth Sports Coaches Association
2050 Vista Parkway
West Palm Beach, FL 33411
www.decatursports.com/articles/NYSCA.htm

Women's Basketball Coaching Association
4646 Lawrenceville Highway
Lilburn, GA 30047
www.wbca.org

Sports Managers and Administrators

T he explosive interest in anything "sports" is clearly reflected in the realm of sports management and administration. Careers range from director of marketing and promotions through assistant general manager and school athletic director to vice president for operations.

Professional Team Positions

Administrative careers not only include those with major league teams, but also the numerous opportunities available with minor league affiliates. Jim Rohr, speaking of his experience as assistant general manager of the Toledo Mud Hens, a Detroit Tigers baseball minor league affiliate, exclaimed, "I love it! I love all aspects of the job, but particularly the people—the fans, the players, the staffs from opposing teams. . . ."

The job includes managing sales, public relations, and marketing for the Hens, which average approximately three thousand fans a game. "This business is difficult to get into—there is very little turnover—but be persistent," Rohr suggested.

Kenny Williams, general manager for the Chicago White Sox, observed, "You've got to be prepared to succeed." Williams, who was selected as one of the top African Americans in sports and athletics by *Sports Illustrated*, worked in several management positions for the Sox before obtaining his present position.

Although the general public already sees him as successful, he feels that unless the team wins, he is not a success! *If you think working for a minor league team lacks electricity and excitement, think again.* The players play hard, the management works hard, and the fans cheer hard. Almost every game, almost every inning, there exists a promotional activity—often contests and free giveaways. The following is a list of the many jobs associated with the Richmond (Virginia) Braves, a minor league affiliate of the Atlanta Braves baseball team:

- General manager
- Associate general manager
- Office manager/Executive secretary
- Field maintenance director
- Director of stadium operation
- Director of ticket operations
- Assistant ticket manager
- Administrative assistants
- Receptionist
- Home clubhouse manager
- Associate home clubhouse manager
- Visiting clubhouse manager
- Umpire room manager
- Radio announcers
- Official scorer
- Public address announcer
- Message center operator
- Scoreboard operator
- Organists
- Interns (lots of interns)

The conclusion: the minor leagues are big time!

The question: how does someone obtain employment in this field?

Currently the preferred route lies through participation in a college program in sports management. A number exist; the following typify contemporary programs. St. Thomas University in Miami, Florida (www.stu.edu), became one of the first institutions to offer a master of science in sports administration. The program prepares students for careers in professional, college, and community sports business, as well as careers in the management of sports facilities. Graduates have entered a variety of careers—traveling secretary, Houston Astros; athletic fund-raiser, University of Houston; assistant executive director, the Orange Bowl; sports information director, University of Tulsa; assistant public relations director, Los Angeles Rams; and arena manager, Yates Field House, Georgetown University.

Courses at St. Thomas include Seminar on Ethics in Sports Administration, Principles of Sports Administration, Legal Aspects of Sports Administration, Sports Financial Management, and others. A major aspect of all such programs is the internship—a chance to work in the sports industry (sometimes paid) as an apprentice. St. Thomas interns have worked for the New York Knicks, the U.S. Olympic Committee, the National Football League office, Hialeah Race Track, Kansas City Parks and Recreation Department, the Nashua (New Hampshire) Pirates, and many others.

Georgia State University also offers a master of science degree in sports administration. The program requires a core of courses, such as Sports Law, Sports Marketing and Promotion, Cultural Aspects of Sports, Budgeting and Finance in Sports and Recreation, and Governance and Ethical Issues in Sports. In addition, students may take electives in a variety of related subjects.

Karen Hargadon Daly typifies students in such programs. A basketball player in high school and college, she wished to continue her interest in sports. She obtained a graduate assistantship at the University of Richmond under successful basketball coach Stephanie Gaitley. She enrolled in a master's degree program in sports management and, following course work and a successful internship with the Philadelphia 76ers NBA basketball team, she graduated. She then landed a job in sports promotions for Trump Castle and Casino, publicizing everything from boxing and professional wrestling to one-on-one basketball contests. Currently, while raising a family, she serves as an adjunct (part-time) professor at Pennsylvania's Widener University in sports marketing.

Most of today's upper-level managers have their college training in management or law. For example, Stan Kastan, president of the Atlanta Braves and the Atlanta Hawks, received his undergraduate degree in psychology and graduate degree in law. However, other managers have had backgrounds ranging from attending business schools to seminaries for clergy. Clearly, there are many paths to leadership positions, but the majority of future leaders will have a college background in sports management.

School and College Sports Administrators

Gerry Kaplan, former athletic director at O'Neil High School in Highland Falls, New York, in many ways typified a successful sports administrator. He started out as a basketball coach and physical education teacher. Upon the retirement of the previous athletic director (AD), he was appointed by the district's board of education to the position of athletic director. In addition to teaching duties as a physical educator, he coached the varsity basketball team. He taught his classes in the early part of the day, leaving the afternoon free for administrative duties—scheduling, attending meetings, coordinating intramurals, and other matters. At smaller schools, the AD may teach several classes; at larger schools, the position may command full-time attention. Hiring, evaluating, and terminating coaches requires many hours in this era of expansion of high school and college interscholastic athletics. Consider also the rainy afternoon when you have to cancel baseball and softball games, a track meet, and a tennis match—then call and notify the games' officials and the bus company to reschedule! If this sounds demanding, consider the athletic director at the University of Texas who lists under his jurisdiction the following areas: business office (tickets and concessions), sports information officer, fund-raiser, athletic trainers, and equipment manager, coaches, athletic dining hall, and stadium supervision. The Texas AD has numerous assistants and strong secretarial support; this is common at the major universities. The position varies with the size of the school or college. Recently, many colleges (and some high schools) have added a director or coordinator of women's athletics. And don't overlook the growing opportunities afforded by community colleges.

Salaries vary widely, averaging between $50,000 and $250,000 a year. The higher figures are earned by athletic directors at large universities with prominent sports programs. The salary is often for twelve months of work, as opposed to the ten-month time commitment of school teachers.

College athletic directors' functions vary with the size of the college and the athletic program. At small (NCAA Division III and NAIA Division II) colleges, they function much like their high school counterparts, and at tiny colleges, they may operate only on a part-time basis. However, NCAA Division I is considered big time—television contracts, game guarantees, major arenas and stadiums, and increased pressure to win. At this level, the AD has a staff of associates and assistants as well as business managers and publicists. Frequently working very long hours, these ADs— some with six-figure salaries—attend many meetings and games; approve contracts; hire and fire; keep the peace among coaches; meet with players, fans, faculty, and alumni; and generally serve as commander in chief. At Yale University, for example, the associate AD performs many functions—one even involves proper and humane burial of horses (Yale has an equestrian team).

Some professional organizations list the abilities necessary in athletic administrators. These include an understanding of:

- the role of athletics in education and our society and the rules, regulations, policies, and procedures of the various governing bodies
- sound business procedures as related to athletic administration
- administrative problems as related to athletic equipment and supplies administration
- problems related to facilities, both indoor and outdoor
- school law and liability
- the factors involved in the conduct of athletic events
- good public relations techniques
- staff relationships
- the health aspects of athletics and the psychological and sociological aspects of sports

Important personality qualities include:

- leadership
- sincere interest in young people and their development
- sense of humor
- even temperament
- optimism
- sense of justice and impartiality
- integrity and solidarity

Some ADs at all levels enter the profession with college-level training in sports management; most, however, are products of physical education administration or sports management programs. Montclair State University in New Jersey offers such a graduate program. Students may concentrate on teaching and administration of physical education, coaching and administration, or exercise sciences. They take such courses as Applied

Sport Psychology, Administration and Supervision of Athletics and Coaching, Orientation to Sports Medicine, and others. College programs vary, including some with similar titles. For example, the sports administration specialty in the physical education master's program at Indiana State University has more of a public relations emphasis. It involves an internship and requires two elective courses outside the program. It does include the following courses: Public Relations in Physical Education and Athletics, Physical Education and the Law, and Social and Psychological Aspects of Sports. Exciting, cutting-edge courses such as those at MSU and ISU make important contributions to future sports administrators.

Park and Recreation Managers

Another specialty within sports administration worthy of consideration is park and recreation management. Arkansas Tech University offers two undergraduate programs:

- **Recreation administration**—prepares students to work in community agency settings and commercial recreation businesses. Programming and people management are major areas of expertise.
- **Park administration**—prepares students to manage large resource areas and visitor facilities. Planning and management aspects of land and water are taught, with private and public recreation and park system management as targeted careers.

Both of these fine programs feature a wide array of courses and an internship. A specialty in this area can be obtained in colleges at the graduate level. For example, the University of Rhode Island, within the master of science in physical education program, offers a specialty in sports and recreation management and recreation education. Students pursue course work in Current Issues in

Physical Education, Health, and Recreation Operations, Sports and Recreation, Principles of Recreation Leadership, and others.

Two important books to read in this regard are *Performance Appraisal for Sports and Recreation Managers* by Joanne MacLean (Human Kinetics) and *Recreational Programming: Designing Leisure Experiences* by Robert Rossman and Barbara Schlatter (Sagamore Publishing).

A good website is www.kaboom.com, which focuses upon playground development and safety.

Finding Your Niche

Sports management is fun, and it's growing, but it also is hard. Not sure if it's for you? Do what Gil Roman did. He served as the part-time business manager for athletics at Jersey City State College while completing his degree in business.

Another sports administration professional who came from a business background—even headed an Internet business (Hoops tv.com)—is Scott O'Neil, now the vice president for business operations and team consulting for the NBA. "I've worked in arena, stadium, and a couple of office buildings," he observed. "I can assure you that the arena—and stadium—is a much better place to drive up to early Monday morning for work." His NBA position is very demanding. "When I walk into an arena, I don't have the luxury of being a fan any more. I'm checking the efficiency of the ticket office, the wait time to enter the arena, security procedures, music selection. . . . The business of sports has given me highs and lows. . . . I wouldn't want it any other way."

All sports programs have business managers. For some, the job is mainly bookkeeping—collecting and paying the bills. For others, a wider variety of duties are performed by a considerable staff. Regardless, it's a good way to break into the field and/or assess the situation.

For More Information

There are a number of resources to turn to for more information, including these three very helpful professional journals in this field:

Athletic Management
Business/Editorial Offices
2488 North Triphammer Road
Ithaca, NY 14850
www.momentummedia.com

Athletics Administration
National Association of Collegiate Directors of Athletics
24651 Detroit Road
Westlake, OH 44145
www.nacda.com

Athletic Business
4130 Lien Road
Madison, WI 53704
www.athleticbusiness.com

CHAPTER THREE

Fitness Careers

A n explosion of interest in physical fitness has taken place in recent years. Well-informed people have learned that overall good health and longevity are directly related to cardio-pulmonary conditioning, weight control, and muscular strength and flexibility. The desire to look marvelous, feel good, and live to a "ripe old age" has resulted in a major boom for the fitness industry.

This fitness boom has resulted in the expansion of opportunities for careers in the following industries: health clubs, sporting goods (such as sneakers and clothing), specialized equipment (including weight-training equipment of all varieties), natural foods and herbs, vitamins and minerals, fitness videos, radio talk shows about medicine and health, relaxation equipment, and related products.

Physical Fitness

Physical fitness takes many forms. While there is some debate over aspects of conditioning and training, most experts agree on the main emphases—weight training, endurance, agility, stretching and running for speed, and cardiovascular development.

Several studies have examined various sports in terms of their contribution to fitness (and, of course, each sport's demands upon the player). Based upon a one-to-ten system, the following list rates various sports according to muscle, lung, and heart requirements.

Auto racing	3	Ice hockey	7
Baseball	3	Judo	7
Basketball	8	Lacrosse	6
Bicycling	4	Marathon	9
Boxing	9	Paddleball	4
Cross-country	6	Relay racing	6
Decathlon	10	Rodeo	3
Field hockey	6	Scuba diving	3
Football	7	Swimming	6
Handball	8	Weight lifting	4

The President's Council on Physical Fitness has developed a similar rating system for the effects of types of exercise, using a scale of zero to twenty-one, as shown in the following chart.

	JOGGING	SWIMMING	BASKETBALL	TENNIS	CALISTHENICS	GOLF	BOWLING
Cardio-respiratory (endurance; stamina)	21	21	19	16	10	8	5
Muscular endurance	20	20	17	16	13	8	5
Muscular strength	17	14	15	14	16	9	5
Flexibility	9	15	13	14	19	8	7
Balance	17	12	16	16	15	8	6
Weight control	21	15	19	16	16	6	5
Muscle definition	14	14	14	13	18	6	5
Digestion	13	13	10	12	11	7	7
Sleep	16	16	12	11	12	6	6

This chart provides information on how demanding the sport(s) of your choice can be, and your training should follow accordingly. Be sure to include a program of flexibility; increased availability of training equipment in recent years has created a sensation in this regard. Likewise, stretching has become part of everyone's program to avoid injury and develop strength.

The trend toward aerobic exercise continues to gain momentum. Aerobic exercises challenge the heart, lungs, and muscles to become stronger and more efficient at the delivery and utilization of oxygen. These routines thus make all of these organs stronger and healthier. In practice, the aerobic exercises utilize the large muscle groups in a repetitive fashion. Common types of aerobic exercise include stationary cycling, stair climbing, stationary rowing, walking, jogging, swimming, cross-country ski machines, and aerobic dance.

Research indicates that when done properly, aerobic activity yields the following positive results:

- promotes strong and healthy bones
- controls the physical and emotional stress in your life
- improves your intellectual capacity and increases your productivity
- helps you to lose fat and keep it off
- provides significant protection from heart disease and stroke
- achieves maximum benefits in a minimum amount of time

"Paying the price," long a slogan in sports, has no greater application than in the area of physical conditioning and training. For some, the price is too great unless looked upon in a positive fashion. That is, the process can be as enjoyable as the result—looking good, feeling good, and living longer and better.

Health Clubs

Following attendance at San Antonio Community College and Cisco Community College in Texas, Jose Bernal found himself behind a computer in an eight-to-five job. Obtaining a transfer, he found improved job satisfaction as a sales representative, largely because he liked working with people. However, not until he joined the staff of President's Health Club in Plano, Texas, teaching aerobics and serving as the club's service manager did he truly enjoy his career.

"I enjoy the real cross section of society that our club attracts, and I like working with people to improve their health," said Bernal. His teaching has included abdominal aerobics, calisthenics, dance, stretching, and a hips-and-thighs routine. Bernal suggested that if you plan to consider his type of career, "you must have a positive personality, be a motivator, and thoroughly like people."

Many centers offer "personal training" for an additional fee. The "personal athletic trainer" provides a program and then closely motivates and monitors the client. This can be done at the latter's home and/or at the club. Julie Victor, personal trainer and co-owner of Vertex Fitness in Bryn Mawr, Pennsylvania, said, "I love my job; I get to work with people every day. They have different concerns and needs. I teach them to move closer to meaningful exercise." Julie feels she is a "human-potential extractor" because, she said, "It's not what you do but how you do it, and how you do anything is how you do everything." Julie participated in a range of sports in high school and college. Moving to her current position was a natural evolution for her.

Hofstra University offers a Personal Trainer/Health Fitness Instructor (CPTHFI) certificate. This is a month-long program that requires students to have prior course work in anatomy and physiology and CPR certification. The course features classroom and practical instruction; students develop both knowledge and skills. Successful completion of the course grants the student the CPTHFI designation. For more information, visit the website at www.hofstrauniversity.edu/ucce.

Not all aerobic instructors work full-time. Stephanie Cugini served part-time at Buena Athletic Club in New Jersey while attending college full-time. "I love aerobics—it gives me a chance to workout, to teach, and I get paid!" she exclaimed. Cugini obtained her certification during a demanding three-day weekend workshop involving evaluation of her knowledge, skills, and teaching effectiveness. The Aerobics and Fitness Association of America organized and conducted the course.

The skills and knowledge of the club employee are critical to the health of the client. Well-trained instructors provide advice to help avoid injury and maximize the benefits of the workout. They also help motivate people to improve their levels of fitness.

Health clubs exist in a variety of geographic settings. The neighborhood mall and the city club are the most common, but others may be in retirement communities, aboard cruise ships, or in large motels and hotels. Corporate fitness/health clubs have also become common. Within this variety, clubs range from the very serious (very expensive)—emphasizing testing and medical evaluation, with specialized programs and rehabilitation, if necessary—to those simply featuring weight-training equipment and aerobic exercise. Accordingly, careers range greatly, from those requiring extensive knowledge and education to those requiring little. Naturally, salaries also vary greatly.

Administrative personnel in the health club industry mirror those of many other commercial enterprises. The major national and regional clubs have a manager, assistant managers, and a regional/district supervisor—and, for national organizations, an executive staff at the corporate office. Independent clubs exist with limited administrative personnel just for the single club. These clubs vary greatly in quality; some are excellent, while others are poor and consequently often fail to survive financially.

At the club level, administrative personnel perform many of the functions of typical service-related industries. They plan budgets; arrange work schedules; hire, evaluate, and dismiss personnel; supervise the maintenance of equipment and wet areas (whirlpool, steam rooms, pool); plan sales quotas; and perform other similar tasks.

In most health clubs, all employees except some specialists have the responsibility to sell memberships. Job performance is often rated to a large degree on this basis. Additionally, sales commissions form an important part of their salaries. Consequently, health club personnel must have excellent sales skills as well as in-depth knowledge of fitness and conditioning.

Corporate Health Clubs

As with commercial health clubs, their corporate counterparts vary widely in sophistication. Some may offer their employees merely a swimming pool or volleyball/basketball courts and a shower facility, while others have the capability of providing medical testing of one's fitness, conducting a monitored program for improvement, and offering education programs such as smoking cessation or relaxation therapy. The trend in the industry leans toward the latter center. Naturally, there is little or no charge to corporate employees for health club memberships, so club workers do not have to sell memberships. If sales is not your thing, this may be a more viable career option.

Corporate fitness centers represent a recent and expanding trend on the health scene. As more enlightened managers and labor leaders realize its value to people and the company, they will include it in collective bargaining agreements for nonmanagerial personnel, as a perk for their executives, and generally as a recruiting tool for prospective employees. Hence, job prospects with corporate health clubs will prove very good.

Exercise physiologists often are hired to manage these facilities. Dr. Ron Feingold, professor of the Department of Physical Education and Human Performance Science at Adelphi University on Long Island, New York, reports that Adelphi's graduate program in exercise physiology has shown excellent growth, attracting students with backgrounds in physical education, nursing, physical therapy, and related areas who all wish to move into this exciting new area.

Some sports medicine centers, such as those associated with hospitals, offer wellness programs to the public. These feature supervised fitness and educational programs similar to corporate centers and require participation fees often paid in part by medical insurance.

Education

Most health club managers have college backgrounds in physical education, exercise physiology, or sports science. For corporate centers, a college degree in a fitness specialty is a must. Obviously, if the club features extensive fitness testing, specialists including medical personnel will be necessary. However, some employees do not need to have a four-year specialized college education, but they do need to acquire the training and knowledge that many people obtain on the job or certification received through a professional organization.

Naturally, appearance remains vital to hiring and retention; you must not only be able to play the part, but also look the part. Perhaps someday you will receive an invitation to join the prestigious National Fitness Leaders Association (listed below) and follow the paths of fitness leaders such as Joe Weider, Judi Sheppard Missett, Denise Austin, Richard Simmons, Dr. Bill Hettler, Jack La Lanne, Joanie Greggains, Cory Everson, and others.

....

For More Information

The following organizations provide information relative to fitness careers:

Aerobics and Fitness Association of America
15250 Ventura Boulevard, Suite 200
Sherman Oaks, CA 91403
www.afaa.com

African American Association of Fitness Professionals
1507 East Fifty-Third Street, Suite 495
Chicago, IL 60615
www.aaafp.org

American Association for Active Lifestyles and Fitness
1900 Association Drive
Reston, VA 20191
www.aahperd.org/aaalf

American Association of Personal Trainers
P.O. Box 11177
Newport Beach, CA 92658
www.aapt.net

American Council on Exercise
4851 Paramount Drive
San Diego, CA 92123
www.acefitness.org

American Fitness Professionals & Associates
P.O. Box 214
Ship Bottom, NJ 08008
www.afpafitness.com

American Society of Exercise Physiologists
Department of Exercise Physiology
College of St. Scholastica
1200 Kenwood Avenue
Duluth, MN 55811
www.asep.org

American Therapeutic Recreation Association
1414 Prince Street, Suite 204
Alexandria, VA 22314
www.atra-tr.org

American Yoga Association
P.O. Box 19986
Sarasota, FL 34276
www.americanyogaassociation.org

Associated Bodywork and Massage Professionals
1271 Sugarbush Drive
Evergreen, CO 80439
www.abmp.com

Association for Worksite Health Promotion
60 Revere Drive, Suite 500
Northbrook, IL 60062

Canadian Association of Fitness Professionals
2851 John Street
P.O. Box 42011
Markham, ON L3R 5R7
Canada
www.canfitpro.com

International Sports Sciences Association
4000 Gutierrez Street
Santa Barbara, CA 93101
www.issaonline.com

National Endurance Sports Trainers Association
29832 Avenida de las Banderas
Rancho Santa Margarita, CA 92688
www.nestacertified.com

National Fitness Leaders Association
5820 Oberlin Drive, Suite 102
San Diego, CA 92121
http://wellness.uwsp.edu/nfla

National School Fitness Foundation
NorthShore Corporate Center, Building II
915 South 500 East, Suite 110
American Fork, UT 84003
www.nsff.net

National Therapeutic Recreation Society
22377 Belmont Ridge Road
Ashburn, VA 20148
www.nrpa.org/index.cfm?publicationid=21

President's Council on Physical Fitness and Sports
Department W
200 Independence Avenue SW, Room 738-H
Washington, DC 202014
www.fitness.gov

CHAPTER FOUR

Sports Officials

*"Without skilled umpires, I knew, the game could not exist. Oh,
players were important, I accepted that, but there were plenty of
players—too many players as far as some umpires were concerned.
But there were only a select few people with the knowledge and
judgment required to control a major league game."*
Ron Luciano, former major league umpire,
in *The Fall of the Roman Umpire*

Officials: they were once the quiet people of sports. Now they
write books, appear on radio and TV talk shows, show militancy, have name recognition among fans, take superiors and
coaches to court, do commercial advertising in print and electronic media—they have joined show business.

For many years, officiating was considered a thankless job in
which the official took verbal abuse—and occasionally physical
abuse—from the coach, players, and crowd. More recently, a
growing respect has been noticeable at all levels for the men and
women who make the game work by enforcing the rules. This
probably has occurred because of growing militancy on the part
of the officials, an increase in their skills, and a realization of their
importance and dedication by the public. Still, a growing feeling
exists among many students of sports that perhaps officials
should return to a less visible role.

Ninety-five percent of all officials serve on a part-time basis,
working mostly with schools and colleges, but also with semi-
professional teams and recreational leagues. Most feel like Peggy

Kershner McKernan, one of the first women to officiate boys' high school basketball, who said, "I love it. It works well with my lifestyle and family obligations, and I enjoy the physical activity and the income it provides."

Earl "Skip" Kingwill, New Jersey sports official, typifies most high school officials. During the day he taught at the elementary level at the Robert Fulton School in the town of North Bergen. At the end of the school day, he left work for the game he had been assigned to as a referee or umpire. Now a retired teacher, he still officiates. In the fall, Earl works almost every day officiating at volleyball matches. In 1999 he was selected as the New Jersey Volleyball Official of the Year. During the winter months, he referees men and women's basketball at the high school and small college levels. He sometimes would ref two games in one day! In the spring, softball occupies his time, umpiring at games and tournaments. Earl's advice to beginning refs: "Establish yourself early in your career as competent; those who do can be assured of earning assignments in tournaments and at higher levels of competition."

Marty Walsh is typical of those who work as officials on a part-time basis. "My officiating background in both football and baseball has been filled with both exciting and rewarding experiences," Walsh commented. He attended the University of Delaware, playing football and baseball, and graduated with a major in biology. During his officiating career in Delaware, Maryland, New Jersey, Pennsylvania, North Carolina, and Virginia, he quickly moved up the ladder. He has officiated numerous championship high school football games and worked many NCAA-IAA college football games; in baseball, he has "umped" high school and college playoff and championship assignments and some minor league professional games. Active in officials' associations, he has served in numerous professional capacities. Noted Walsh, "I feel the friendships I've developed and my professional growth are invaluable by-products of this avocation."

The schedule of the official is not for everyone. Weekdays see them scurrying from their full-time positions to contests; weekends, likewise, prove hectic as the officials work games on Saturdays and, in some leagues, even on Sundays!

Many officials earn their livelihoods as educators. Others own their own businesses or work flexible hours in careers such as sales so as to be available for afternoon sporting events.

While most view the profession as an avocation, a select few make it to the inner circle of full-time professional officials. These individuals normally pay their dues as did Marty Walsh: by gaining several years of experience at the lower levels, such as high school, college, and the minor leagues.

Richie Powers, in his classic book *Overtime* (Ballantine), provided an excellent look at the life of a professional basketball official in the National Basketball Association. He wrote: "I'm usually quick with the whistle and even quicker with my thumb, in the area of technical fouls, but I set a record tonight by calling my first technical of the season less than two minutes into the game. Manny [Sokol] had called a foul against Phil Chenier of the Bullets. Instead of rolling the ball to Manny, or at least bouncing it toward him, Chenier held it defiantly, glaring in Manny's direction. Then he flipped the ball out of bounds. Tweet! I hit him with a technical foul for unsportsmanlike conduct. . . . Listen, I call technical fouls in an attempt to maintain control of the game."

Obviously, the emotional control of officials is tested many times in each game!

Officiating Guidelines

The following guidelines (almost requirements) have been prepared by *Referee* magazine focus on the most important things for officials to remember:

- **Be competitive.** The players give maximum effort, and so should you. Tell yourself, "I'm not going to let this game get away from me. I am better than that." You are hired to make the calls that control the game—make them!

- **Have your head on right.** Don't think your striped shirt grants you immunity from having to take a little criticism. It's part of officiating. Plan on it. Successful officials know how much to take. Ask one when you get the chance.
- **Don't be a tough guy.** If a coach is on your back, but not enough to warrant a penalty, then stay away from him (or her). This is especially true during time-outs. Standing near an unhappy coach just to "show him" will only lead to further tensions. Some officials develop irritating characteristics. Don't be one of them.
- **Get into the flow of the game.** Each game is different. Good officials can feel this difference. Concentrate on the reactions of the players. Take note if the tempo of the game changes. A ragged game calls for a different style of officiating than a smooth one.
- **Don't bark.** If you don't like to be shouted at, don't shout at someone else. Be firm, but speak with a normal, relaxed voice. This technique will do wonders in helping you reduce the pressure. Shouting indicates a loss of control, not only of one's self, but also of the game.
- **Show confidence.** Cockiness has absolutely no place in officiating. You want to exude confidence. Your presence should command respect from the participants. As in any walk of life, appearance, manner, and voice determine how you are accepted. Try to present the proper image.
- **Forget the fans.** As a group, fans exhibit three common characteristics: (1) ignorance of the rules, (2) highly emotional partisanship, and (3) delight in antagonizing the officials. Accepting these facts will help you ignore the fans, unless they interrupt the game or stand in the way of your doing your job.
- **Answer reasonable questions.** Treat coaches and players in a courteous way. If they ask you a question reasonably, answer them in a polite way. If they get your ear by saying, "Hey, Ref, I want to ask you something," and then start

telling you off, interrupt and remind them of the reason for the discussion. Be firm, but relaxed.

- **Choose your words wisely.** Don't aggressively threaten coaches or players. This will only put them on the defensive. More important, you will have placed yourself on the spot. If you feel a situation is serious enough to warrant a threat, then it is serious enough to penalize, without invoking a threat. Obviously some things you say will be a form of threat, but using the proper words can make it subtle.

- **Stay cool.** Your purpose is to establish a calm environment for the game. Nervous or edgy officials are easily spotted by fans, coaches, and players alike. Avoid chewing gum, pacing around, or displaying a wide range of emotions prior to or during a game; this will make you seem vulnerable to the pressure.

The above suggestions, generally applicable to officiating at all levels, may need slight modification in special situations. However, as a whole, they provide useful guidelines. Excellent mechanics and a thorough knowledge of the rules are an important part of being a truly successful official. But establishing and maintaining rapport with coaches and players also help officials avoid many potentially difficult situations.

One researcher, Dr. Roy Askins, a professor of social psychology with officiating experience, examined his hobby and provided the following information. When asked, "What gives officials the most trouble?" Dr. Askins replied that "other than problems associated with perception and sloppy plays, the behavior of some coaches, players, and crowds is most troublesome."

At this point, you may ask, "If officiating is so demanding in terms of working conditions, why do people do it?" A survey administered by Dr. Askins found many reasons. The most common were earning extra money, remaining close to athletics in some capacity, and enjoying a position of status and power. If you think this career looks promising for you, make plans to begin.

Getting Started

What kind of person makes a good sports official? Dr. R. C. Haygood, a vocational psychologist at Arizona State University, said that the ideal sports official would be a saint, for only a saint could exhibit all of the psychological traits we expect of a good referee or umpire! Some of these personality characteristics are tolerance, self-confidence, and the ability to make decisions under stress. There's one way to see if you possess these: give officiating a try.

"Sometimes, I look back and I just can't believe it. I am thirty-four. I am a black woman. I referee in the NBA," said Violet Palmer in a January 2000 interview in *Referee* magazine. She attributes her quick rise to the pros to her career as a player (high school, college) and to attending camps for referees. She officiated in high school for one year, and then several college conferences hired her—she quickly moved to top conferences and top games, including the Women's NCAA Final Four. Until then it was all women's games. Finally, she attended several NBA officials' camps, and then on October 31, 1997, she refereed her first pro game. She has been a mainstay ever since.

While Violet officiates in the Men's NBA, Eddie Malloy is breaking into the Women's NBA (WNBA) and Men's NBA. Eddie began his career officiating Catholic Youth Organization (CYO) elementary basketball games. Later he moved to high school and summer league action. However, part of his summer he devotes to attending officiating camps—"They are a bit costly, but they pay off." Currently, he officiates the WNBA/NBA on a part-time basis, and he hopes to move up to full-time status. "I try to work out regularly at a health club because refs have to be in excellent physical condition, and of course I want to look good in the uniform."

If you're interested, volunteer to officiate in a youth summer league, in a church or synagogue league in your neighborhood, or in the community recreation program. Many league officers at this level go begging for officials! Your involvement can aid both yourself and the league; some youth leagues and intramural programs even provide salaries, but your greatest benefit will be experience. In addition, officiating is an excellent way to better understand a sport; it will give you a greater appreciation of the total game as well as a working knowledge of the rules. This serves as a valuable background for related careers.

If you become seriously interested, it's useful to remember that officiating parallels coaching in many respects. That is, novices work with younger players at the lower level. So, following approval, you usually will work games at the junior high school and junior varsity levels. In order to receive initial status, it will be necessary to pass a written examination in the sport or sports of your choice and to join the state officials' association as well as the local chapter.

During the probationary period, usually a couple of years, the newcomer will come under the observation of senior officials for evaluation. They look for a good working knowledge of the game, combined with several abilities, such as how well he or she performs in stressful situations. As new officials improve their skills, they are asked to work more games and are promoted to higher-level games, perhaps even important tournaments or championship events. Naturally, salaries improve with the level officiated. They also vary with geographic location.

Some officials want to move on to the college level. This involves joining another association, taking a test, and proving oneself again. College officials receive very good per-game salaries, and most conferences also pay travel expenses.

One major college conference listed its requirements for applicants for officials' positions: less than forty years of age when applying, in good physical condition, and able to pass an exam. These requirements must be met, and three ability references must be submitted. While a high school diploma is necessary, a college degree is preferred. In addition, the person must have employment and residence in close proximity to the conference.

The candidate's day job has to permit flexibility so the official is free for travel and games. While some background as a player is desirable, the officiating experience must include eight to ten years at the high school level plus approximately four years in a comparable conference. If these criteria appear too demanding, remember that most positions will not be this difficult to obtain—the above requirements represent a special situation for one of the nation's premier conferences.

Officiating Schools

Although a study of the readership of *Referee* magazine indicated that most officials became introduced to their profession by a friend or through participation in sports, many future officials probably will enter the career as a result of attendance at a school. The officials' associations provide training programs for new recruits; the schools, however, represent an in-depth, concentrated approach to learning the officials' art. Some master officials conduct annual conferences for officials. These clinics, usually two-day meetings, exist for officials of all levels who wish to improve their skills.

The following serve as typical examples of the schools available. One of the nation's best-known and most popular programs is the Harry Wendelstedt School for Umpires. The specific purpose is to supply supervised training for young people to qualify for umpire positions in professional, college, high school, semipro, and sandlot baseball. The school, which meets for six weeks, runs from directly after the New Year's holiday until early February. The program follows this schedule: Classes begin at 8:30 A.M. with a ninety-minute session that explains and tests the student's knowledge of the rules and situations that actually confront umpires. At 10:30 A.M., the class reports to the playing fields, where a program of exercises and conditioning takes place. Following this, a series of practice drills provides instruction in proper mechanics—stance, voice control, positions, and others. Each student receives instruction and practice in all phases of umpiring. After the completion of the first ten days of school, the late afternoons—3:30 P.M. until 6:00 P.M.—are spent working high school and college games. No jobs are promised, but many of Wendelstedt's graduates have entered the profession at all levels. Some (approximately fifteen) exceptional students do receive appointments directly after finishing the school, and many are called at a later date. This school has trained the majority of the officials in blue working in the majors today. If this sounds interesting, write for additional information to:

Harry Wendelstedt School for Umpires
88 South St. Andrews Drive
Ormond Beach, FL 32174
www.umpireschool.com

One graduate, Ed Barycki, decided to attend the school after working a few softball games: "The umpiring bug bit me, and I went to Harry's just wanting to learn, and I ended up the top graduate in the class!" Following graduation, Barycki worked in the South Atlantic League, then in the Carolina League (both affiliates of major league baseball). However, he missed the time away from his home and family. He gave up his attempt to make it to the "bigs." However, he stayed within the profession by moonlighting as an umpire for major college games on the East Coast.

Other schools for umpires include:

Brinkman-Froemming Umpire School
1021 Indian River Drive
Cocoa, FL 39222

Jim Evans Academy of Professional Umpiring
12741 Research Boulevard, Suite 401
Austin, TX 78750
www.umpireacademy.com

Typical learning experiences at officiating schools include:

* in-depth examination of the current *Official Baseball Rule Book*
* home-plate mechanics, including timing, voice control, and positioning
* instruction in moral conduct
* proper use of fair and foul signals by base and home-plate umpires
* extensive use of video aids
* guest lectures
* practice, practice, practice of umpiring skills

Each summer, Nationwide Basketball Referee's Camp hosts many active and aspiring officials. The three-day sessions attract people from all over the country. The camp format begins with morning presentations, films, and lectures. Topics such as floor mechanics, what type of officials supervisors look for at higher levels, personality traits of successful officials, and proper use of signals form some of the content of the course.

Following lunch, the refs work games of high school players attending a nearby camp. Each one receives an evaluation of the game he or she officiates. Evenings find the students actively officiating; each ref participates in four games daily. At the conclusion of camp, each person receives an honest appraisal of her or his ability. The refs attend to expand their knowledge and skills with the hope that they can improve the level of games they work. Many do profit and move up; others may need further improvement that comes through experience. If you wish additional information, contact:

Nationwide Basketball Referees Camp
c/o Men's Basketball Office
University of Massachusetts
Amherst, MA 01003

Other sports also offer similar schools, clinics, and summer camps. An example of a school for hockey officials is:

Canadian School of Hockey Officiating
265 Rimrock Road, Unit 4
Toronto, ON M3J 3C6
Canada
www.refschool.com

Other camps, schools, and clinics include:

Rocky Mountain Football Officials Camp
2300 Fourteenth Avenue South, #10
Great Falls, MT 59405

Coast to Coast Referee School
P.O. Box 412
Ellenton, FL 34222
   The clinic is held in Dallas, Texas.

MEAC Basketball Camp
102 North Elm Street, Suite 104
Greensboro, NC 27401

Professional Referee Observation School
3230 Durham Drive
Riverside, CA 92503

Eric Gregg, in his book *Working the Plate: The Eric Gregg Story*, suggested that umpires in the minors not marry—they cannot afford it. Salaries for umpires in these leagues remain very poor. (Undoubtedly, this contributed to Ed Barycki's decision to give up the minor league life.) According to the Major League Baseball Umpire Development Program, salaries for minor league umpires ranged from $2,000 to $3,400 per month in 1997.

Opportunities exist in all areas for officials, but particularly in women's sports, certain nonrevenue sports, and with some college conferences. Salaries range widely; most officials earn approximately $50 to $150 per game for high school major varsity sports and from $150 to $500 (with major conferences paying more) at the college level. Professional salaries vary with the sport and the number of games.

The expansion of sports at all levels and the growth of women's participation guarantee opportunities for new officials. For energetic people willing to work hard and master all the rules of a given sport, this can be a promising part-time or even full-time career area.

Start Your Future Now

If officiating is potentially your career, pursue these suggestions:

1. Read about your future profession. Subscribe to *Referee* magazine—it contains excellent information, updates, current happenings, profiles of successful officials, and suggestions for improving your skills. For a subscription, write to:

   Referee
   P.O. Box 161
   Franksville, WI 53126

   Examine the following website designed for sports officials—www.rightstaff.com—and that of the National Association of Sports Officials—www.naso.org. Also read books on officiating, such as Richie Power's *Overtime* (Ballantine), Kathryn Davis' *The Art of Sports Officiating* (Allyn and Bacon), John McDonough's *Don't Hit Him, He's*

Dead (Celestial Arts), Edward Dolan's *Calling the Play: A Beginner's Guide to Amateur Sports Officiating* (Atheneum), and Eric Gregg and Marty Appel's *Working the Plate: the Eric Gregg Story* (William Morrow).

2. Volunteer to officiate, wherever you can find an opportunity. Many exist. What you don't earn in salary you will in experience.

3. Study and master the rules for your sport. Stay aware of recent changes, interpretations, and emphases. The NCAA and high school athletic associations provide rule books.

4. Participate to the extent you are able in the sport of your interest.

5. Work to develop the personality traits of an official, such as independence, maturity, self-confidence, and a high moral character.

6. Study your sport's officials. Use your imagination and make the calls. It will be good practice. Read technical books on officiating and on your sport.

7. Write to the administrative office of the league you might like to officiate for and ask the requirements so you can begin to prepare. Each league (at all levels) has a person performing the task of supervising and assigning officials. For example, for professional baseball, contact:

Office for Baseball Umpire Development
P.O. Box A
225 Fourth Street
St. Petersburg, FL 33731

8. Most important: follow the Code of Ethics, reprinted on the following page, from the National Federation of Officials Association, an affiliate of the National Federation of State High School Associations.

CODE OF ETHICS

- Officials shall master both the rules of the game and the mechanics necessary to enforce the rules, and shall exercise authority in an impartial, firm and controlled manner.

- Officials shall work with each other and their state associations in a constructive and cooperative manner.

- Officials shall uphold the honor and dignity of the profession in all interaction with student-athletes, coaches, athletic directors, school administrators, colleagues, and the public.

- Officials shall prepare themselves both physically and mentally, shall dress neatly and appropriately, and shall comport themselves in a manner consistent with the high standards of the profession.

- Officials shall be punctual and professional in the fulfillment of all contractual obligations.

- Officials shall remain mindful that their conduct influences the respect that student-athletes, coaches and the public hold for the profession.

- Officials shall, while enforcing the rules of play, remain aware of the inherent risk of injury that competition poses to student-athletes. Where appropriate, they shall inform event management of conditions or situations that appear unreasonably hazardous.

- Officials shall take reasonable steps to educate themselves in the recognition of emergency conditions that might arise during the course of competition.

CHAPTER FIVE

Sports Communicators

The field of sports communication teems with opportunities. Jobs become available daily with newspapers, radio, and television because professional and college teams engage large numbers of people. In "sports show business," sports communicators rank near the top in the world in glamour, sheer fun and excitement, and oftentimes, financial rewards. Within the field numerous careers exist.

Sportswriters

Dramatic contrasts exist in newspaper careers. Paul Smith has written for a variety of newspapers, including the *Harrisburg Patriot*, the *Wilmington-News Journal*, the *Philadelphia Journal*, the *Philadelphia Inquirer*, the *Pittsburgh Press*, and currently the *News-Dispatch* in Michigan City, Indiana. Smith has enjoyed assignments such as covering the Chicago Cubs and White Sox during the baseball season; Notre Dame football in the fall; and Indiana, Purdue, and Notre Dame during the basketball season, as well as local sporting events. His advice to aspiring writers: "The romantic bloom comes off the rose early in the profession, but if you stick with it, it has its rewards."

Contrast Smith's meandering with Tony Leodora, former sports editor at the *Times Herald* in Norristown, Pennsylvania, who served over fifteen years with one newspaper. Following college,

Leodora took a position in business but was able to pursue his life-long interest in sports through working part-time at the newspaper as a stringer (correspondent) who attended local events and wrote about them for the paper. Eventually Leodora decided to go full-time, and upon the retirement of the sports editor, he was promoted to that position.

Leodora's schedule varied. Mornings found him in the office; afternoons were free except when he had an interview or game to cover. Evenings found him covering an athletic event and then often returning to the office to write up his story and coordinate the sports pages. Other times he was able to send his story to the paper via computer. He got excellent seats at all athletic events, met regularly with professional sports stars and coaches, occasionally traveled to events in other cities—and got paid for it all! In particular, he loved baseball spring training in Florida. But it was not all fun and games. There were many long days, and writing is hard (though enjoyable) work.

For many years, some of the finest journalism has been found on the sports pages of America's papers. It is here that lively, fast-paced, colorful action writing appears. Some sportswriters have become well-known for adopting a uniquely aggressive style, such as Christie "Jock Talk" Blatcheard of the *Toronto Financial Post*, T. J. Simers of the *Los Angeles Times*, Phil Mushnick of the *New York Post*, Mike Lupica and Dick Weiss of the *New York Daily News*, and Bill Conlon of the *Philadelphia Daily News*. The size, circulation, and location of the paper determine to a large degree the activities of the sportswriters. The sports department of a small-town newspaper normally has an editor, one other writer, and perhaps a couple of part-timers who cover local weekend events. Such a paper relies upon the wire services (such as the Associated Press) for national stories.

A large-city daily may have a sports staff of ten; several of these individuals have a particular specialty, such as golf, football, boxing, or the high school scene. While these reporters cover other events during the off-season, they write several articles a week related to their expertise when their sport is underway. Some write columns a couple of times a week.

Frequently, reporters work unusual hours and days. For example, those employed by a morning newspaper usually work late afternoon and evening hours, five days a week, including Saturdays (if there's a Sunday edition). They then would have two weekdays off. Major papers will send a reporter along with the team to cover out-of-town stories. While this sounds glamorous, it frequently is time consuming and hectic. Following the event, the writer uses his or her notes to prepare the article, looking for a particular angle or interesting aspect to highlight for reader appeal. The writer calls in the completed article (usually preparing and sending it via computer) and finally gets to sleep, usually about 2:00 A.M.

As a sportswriter, you receive a lot of free tickets, but newspapers remain notorious for paying mediocre salaries to their professionals, and smaller papers pay even less. Of course, it's possible that you will gain a reputation and be given your own column, which could lead to a more substantial income. Having a column means that your work appears regularly in the same location in the paper, usually under your photograph. Your column would be commentary rather than straight reporting, and in terms of your career, a column marks your success as a sportswriter.

Preparing for Your Sportswriting Career

Many opportunities exist on small, local, and weekly newspapers to begin your career. If a vacancy does not exist in sports, take a position writing news; it will help you build your writing skills and will aid you in making a switch to sports when an opening occurs.

At one time, reporters began their careers as copy aides, helping around the office by performing clerical tasks. Having proven themselves reliable, they might be asked to join the staff as cub reporters. This would involve small, unspectacular assignments eventually leading up to important tasks. Today, few sportswriters start this way. Most attend college and pursue course work in the department or school of journalism or communication arts. If you plan such a career, include several courses in writing; grammar skills will be a necessity. You also should consider building a strong background in the humanities and using your free electives in sports courses from the physical education program. Courses in photography will increase your chances of obtaining a job, particularly with smaller papers.

Sportswriter Jackie Lopin suggested that while you're in your last two years of college, you should make an especially strong effort to land a summer or part-time job on the local newspaper; constant new experiences are the key to becoming a good sportswriter. These experiences will greatly enhance your ability to obtain a full-time position following graduation.

Characteristics of Sportswriting

In recent years, the expansion of television and radio coverage of sporting events has resulted in a modification of newspaper coverage. A decline in straight factual reporting and an increase in features has occurred. Not only does the reader want to know what happened, but also such additional information as the condition of the player injured, who might be traded, and the likelihood of the team's success against the next opponent. However, most common in features are interviews with athletes answering a series of questions about aspects of their careers.

Despite its outward appearance, the life of a newspaper person has its lonely side. In fact, one observer found that "creative loneliness" is an important characteristic of successful writers. After the big game or press conference, the hard work of writing, editing, and rewriting must be completed alone—and prior to the deadline!

A newspaper writer has a very special obligation to society to remain vigilant for excesses that may destroy sports. Some outstanding features have resulted from careful, excellent investigative research revealing serious abuses in sports. Too frequently, athletes, coaches, and administrators have engaged in conduct detrimental to their own profession for personal benefit. Coaches have forced injured players to participate; athletic directors have condoned illegal recruiting; players have put their own importance above that of their team and their sport; youth league managers have played only to win; and coaches have publicly abused players for mistakes. Even some parents unduly pressure their children to be superstars. It is here that the writer can make an important contribution.

Career Opportunities for Sportswriters

The number of big-city papers has diminished in recent years; however, many papers have expanded, and many others have begun in new locations. Opportunities exist for well-prepared and knowledgeable candidates. In considering this career, sportswriter Jackie Lopin has said that sometimes it's glamorous, usually it's exciting, and always it's very hard work. Even the writers considered the best in the country will tell you that it took years and years of dedicated effort to develop their craft.

There are a number of career options for sportswriters beyond newspapers. Here is a brief look at other media that require good writers who are interested in sports.

Books. Many writers also produce books as a sideline. This serves as a creative outlet for their talents as well as an additional source of income. A considerable market exists for sports books, and publishers often look for manuscripts from newspaper people. Sportswriters commonly coauthor books with sports figures. For example, Dick Weiss, *New York Daily News*, has authored the following: *Full-Court Pressure: A Year in Kentucky Basketball* (with Rick Pitino), *Refuse to Lose* (with John Calipari), *Campus Chaos: Why the Game I Love Is Breaking My Heart* (with Dick Vitale), and others.

Magazines. The growth of national, regional, and specialty magazines provides a ready market for the sportswriter. While major periodicals *(Sports Illustrated, Inside Sports)* have full-time staffs, they often utilize freelancers for specialty pieces. *Sporting News* and similar national newspapers make extensive use of purchased articles. Although less lucrative, regional magazines buy manuscripts, as do a host of specialty publications—sports yearbooks, college and professional football and basketball game programs, professional and minor league game programs, college and professional media guides, and others. Specific sport magazines— *Volleyball, Muscle & Fitness, Soccer Digest, Hockey Player, Golf Digest, Skiing Magazine, Swim Magazine, Tennis Magazine,* and many, many others—provide additional outlets. National publications of a general nature—such as *Parade Magazine*—often run sports stories. If you wish to write and have the necessary skills, you should be able to find a format and an outlet.

Internet. The World Wide Web has provided many opportunities for writers to showcase their ideas. As with magazines, Internet outlets vary in article requirements, prestige, and remuneration. A couple of years ago, as the Internet blossomed, Craig Dimitri, a sport enthusiast, contacted Vusports.com, part of Rivals.com, to offer his services covering Villanova University basketball. Rivals.com is a private national organization that largely focuses on college and sometimes high school sports (largely football and basketball). Craig was hired and now sits courtside as he reports on Villanova sporting events. For him it's an avocation that he performs part-time; his day job is as a lawyer.

Eric Germunder has a great interest in football, particularly the NCAA, I-AA college teams and their conferences. For several years he has written an excellent newsletter that appears each Thursday beginning in August (season preview) and continuing through the football season on his website, where he also posts links related to I-AA football. It's also e-mailed to subscribers. "I love doing it; it's fun, a real labor of love," Eric said. As with other careers and avocations in sports (photography, statistics, umpiring), often a hobby can translate to a job.

Thousands and thousands of websites cover virtually every aspect of sports and athletics. All major sports organizations—from ESPN (www.espn.com) and *Sporting News* (www.sporting news.com) to *Sports Illustrated* (www.sportsillustrated.com) and NASCAR (www.nascar.com)—maintain active websites. These sites require frequent updating, sometimes hourly, and writers are needed for this.

Sportscasters

Sports talk show hosts have swept over North America, settling down in every locale. They have fan support and strong ratings. Most large cities in North America can boast of sports talk shows. Many even have all-sports radio stations with round-the-clock sports talk hosts, most of them excellent. In addition, national shows have appeared (and disappeared). ESPN radio has stations around the country and a growing listenership.

The growth of sports talk radio has reached phenomenal proportions. Founded in the 1970s by sports talk giants—such as Art Rusk Jr. (WABC-AM), Don Henderson (WCAU-AM), Ira Faistel and later Lisa Bowman (KABC-AM), and Pete Franklin (WWWE-AM)—sports-based radio programs have become immensely popular. Not a substitution by a coach or a call by an umpire goes unchallenged by fans. Occasionally, the fans who phone in operate from a lack of knowledge about the essence or subtleties of the sport involved and, when challenged, become highly emotional and irrational, adding to the shows' interest. Some stations are rumored to have banned certain callers!

Characteristics of Sportscasting

Trends marking the industry include a move away from the once-popular insult-screaming host toward the calmer, knowledgeable professional and the use of a cohost. The latter trend opens the door for a rookie to join with an experienced partner, making for a successful show. The best talk broadcasts combine commentary by the broadcaster about the performance of local teams and players, interviews with interesting sports personalities, and telephone calls from listeners. A show with a theme, frequently utilizing editorial comments by the host as a springboard, seems to work best. Howard Eskin (WIP-AM) is a model in this regard, beginning his show with a controversial and timely topic and then letting the callers go ballistic! This job requires excellent knowledge of many sports, as the broadcaster frequently is put on the spot, and it is only for people who love athletics. Broadcasters in their time off often attend games, practices, and press conferences. Some handle sports news for their stations in addition to their shows. Mike Francessa and Chris "Mad Dog" Russo (WFAN 660) are considered by many as the top team in the business. They combine knowledge and enthusiasm as the "old pro" (Mike) jousts with the callers, guests, and his emotional partner (Chris). Many women also run shows, although usually not in prime time.

Undoubtedly the best way to break in as a sports talk show host involves starting in a smaller market or working first as a sports journalist. These shows frequently hire newspaper people part-time for weekends as well as for full-time positions.

Radio provides jobs in sports in addition to the talk show positions. Most major stations have a sports editor, providing news and often commentary. And thousands of stations across the nation broadcast athletic events live. Professional, college, and high school games need announcers who understand the sport and can communicate the action clearly and colorfully. Normally, one individual provides play-by-play, while the other gives analysis.

Successful radio broadcasting can result in a move to the big time and big money—television! A magnificent book that comes with two audio CDs provides a wonderful review of this career and its contribution to sports: *And the Crowd Goes Wild: Relive the Most Celebrated Sporting Events Ever Broadcast* (Sourcebooks).

Television announcers receive the best salaries and the greatest exposure to the public. They may be employed by a sports team or a TV station—or both. Some serve as the sports reporter on the station's news program. As such, they cover many areas, necessitating a good knowledge of at least the major sports. Although they may appear on the show only twice a day for four or five minutes, TV sportscasters spend most of the day preparing for their air time. Often this involves attending press conferences, interviewing players, and covering games. It's an exciting life that brings the sportscaster in close contact with the athletic world. Many have a chance to try automobile racing, playing quarterback (in practice), and pitching batting practice as a promotion. These activities are arranged to increase viewer interest and to expand the announcer's credibility as someone knowledgeable about sports.

The growth of cable television, such as ESPN and a variety of local and regional stations, has expanded opportunities in television. Like network and local commercial stations, cable operators need game announcers, producers, program directors, hosts for interview shows and panel discussions, announcers to report game results, and interviewers for news stories, human interest pieces, and investigative reports.

Some sports announcers have captured the attention of the public. Brent Musburger's career moves, John Madden's fear of flying, and Tim McCarver's honest criticism of players have made headlines. In general, game announcers capture the most attention. As with radio, they fall into two categories: play-by-play or color specialists. The play-by-play announcer generally explains each play as it occurs and its relationship to the overall game. The color commentator, usually a former player, provides insights into certain techniques and strategies the coach or athletes may employ; he or she often provides amusing anecdotes about players. Most recently there has been an attempt to carefully put together a team of announcers who complement each other's abilities and contribute to the listeners' enjoyment of the game.

Staff people spend many hours preparing for a game or event. Studying players' backgrounds, talking with coaching staffs, and meeting with public relations specialists help in this regard. Sometimes a third person contributes to announcing a nationally telecast game.

Beginning Your Sportscasting Career

Knowledge of sports and an excellent speaking voice are important prerequisites for a career in sportscasting. Writing skills are also essential, since most sportscasters compose the information they announce. Physical attractiveness looms important for the television positions.

Donna de Varona, a TV sports communicator, cautioned that you should have both a sports and an academic background; it's very hard for someone who has never played or been on the line in a competitive sport to really understand the dynamics of the game. Therefore, it is useful to take many of the same courses suggested for newspaper and public relations careers, such as writing and public speaking, as well as sports studies and physical education. Similarly, try to become involved in sports at some level of activity.

If you do not wish to perform in front of the camera or a microphone, careers exist in the background. For example, technical personnel are needed to operate cameras. Producers plan show content, timing, and commercials. Positions as broadcast technicians also exist in radio and television. These individuals operate and maintain the electronic equipment responsible for transmitting the signals onto the airwaves.

If you did not attend college (or even if you did), consider attending a trade school designed for radio and television careers. These schools offer short, intensive courses and assist with job placement. If you wish additional information, contact the following organization with your request for a list of the schools in your area:

Career College Association
10 G Street NE, Suite 750
Washington, DC 20002
www.career.org

For those interested in the world of sports broadcasting, consider attending a broadcasting school. A typical curriculum features classroom instruction, live practice, guest lectures, broadcasting, and critique sessions.

The Connecticut School of Broadcasting, which offers courses in several states, prepares students for entry-level careers, including on-air and behind-the-scenes work. Such positions include but are not limited to the following: audio and video production, studio operations, sales, talk show hosting, sportscasting, and others. For more information, contact:

Connecticut School of Broadcasting
Radio Park
Farmington, CT 06032
http://800tvradio.com

Two sportscasting institutes are offered by Hofstra University for a week each August: "Introduction to Sportscasting for Teens" and "Summer Broadcasting Institute for Adults." The latter offers both instruction and practice and several guest lectures from prominent sportscasters. For more information, contact:

University College for Continuing Education
250 Hofstra University
Hempstead, NY 11549
www.hofstra.edu/ucce

Once you have obtained the necessary education, consider this suggestion from Keith Jackson of ABC-TV's "Wide World of

Sports": If you want to be a television sportscaster, begin where you are comfortable. You shouldn't be too eager to run for the big city when the smaller community affords the better learning experience.

Many, many opportunities exist at the thousands of radio and hundreds of television stations in North America. Here the novice can hone skills and learn the art of the professional. Some individuals so enjoy their jobs in small towns and cities that they stay and make it a career. Others use this background as a springboard to the "big time."

For additional information on sports journalism, contact:

National Association of Broadcasters
1771 N Street NW
Washington, DC 20036
www.nab.org

Talkshowhosts.com
2791 South Buffalo Drive
Las Vegas, NV 89117
www.talkshowhosts.com

National Sportscasters and Sportswriters Association
322 East Innes Street
Salisbury, NC 28144
www.nssahalloffame.com

Sports Public Relations Specialists

The dramatic growth of sports public relations (PR) stems from two perspectives: first, the desire by the fans and the media to learn more—and more, and more—about their teams and their favorite players, and second, the desire by colleges and professional teams to develop and/or maintain favorable opinions of their organizations or institutions.

Public relations specialists work to obtain publicity to fill stadiums, increase the visibility of colleges, and promote players. The activities vary with the size of the college or organization. For professional teams, the public relations program varies with the team level; major league team agents are busier than those at the lower levels. Another factor that affects this office's work is the success of the team and its players. Playoff teams and those with superstars create great interest and consequently test the energies of the PR staff.

The work setting is usually superior for professional and major college sports public relations specialists. Offices feature comfortable arrangements with the latest equipment, and the seats at the games are prime.

At the major college level (Division I), the PR director is supported by assistants, a secretary, and a few interns (those studying for the profession). Sports information director (SID) is the title most utilized in colleges for this position. However, some schools are now using the title director of media relations for athletics.

At the professional level, teams normally have a public relations staff consisting of a director, an assistant, a secretary, and a few interns. Smaller colleges have a one-person office, a part-time person, or none at all.

One of the most enjoyable aspects of the job is the opportunity to watch the game. Of course, pregame preparations are involved; for example, preparing news releases, compiling statistics, issuing credentials to the media covering the event, arranging refreshments, and hosting VIPs. Some typical activities follow:

- **Prepare media guides.** Produce booklets containing information on players and teams as well as statistics and records for the sport and, at the professional level, team yearbooks and related materials. Produce and distribute annual highlight videos. At some schools and for some sports, provide video to local television stations; this provides coverage for a team or event.

- **Arrange or conduct media briefings.** Meetings with newspaper writers and TV and radio reporters bring them information about a player or team development.
- **Coordinate press conferences.** Meet with the media for the coach and/or players.
- **Send news releases to media.** Usually two or three pages both before and after the game provide new information and statistics for newspapers, radio, and TV.
- **Send specific news releases.** These provide information and photographs to players' hometown newspapers.
- **Maintain files.** Collect information, including historical and statistical data, on athletes and teams.
- **Direct the press box.** For certain sports, arrange for seating and materials for newspaper, radio, and television representatives, as well as for distribution of admission credentials.
- **Maintain a scrapbook.** Clip newspaper items about the teams and players.
- **Provide and arrange for photography.** Arrangements for a photograph of each player (head-and-shoulders portrait called a mug shot) must be made, along with team photos and action video for TV; videotape highlights and photographs are made available to the media.
- **Answer requests.** Give information to the league office, NCAA/NAIA office, other teams, and the general public.
- **Write stories.** Not all newspapers send reporters to cover an event, so a story often is written by the sports publicist and distributed to the press. In recent years, this job has expanded to writing a postgame Web story complete with statistics very shortly following the event.

If this position sounds demanding, you're right. Many days you work from 9 A.M. to midnight! When the team is on the road, a sports publicist goes, too. This may be a trip to the Rose Bowl in Pasadena or to the Maui Invitational Basketball Tournament in

Hawaii, but it more frequently means a five-hour bus ride to less glamorous cities or towns.

Discussing her role as senior vice president for communications for ESPN, PR pro Rosa Gatti said, "The primary objective of my department is to attain the most extensive and favorable exposure for the company in the media, in order to attract public interest in the network and, in particular, viewing of the network's telecasts."

Before joining ESPN, Gatti served as the first woman sports information director at a major college in the United States. She was named to this position at Villanova University and later held a similar position at Brown University. During this time, she held two executive positions: president of the Eastern College Athletic Conference (ECAC) and vice president of the College Sports Information Directors of America. She likewise paid her dues on many game days. She followed this rigorous schedule on Saturdays in the fall:

7:30 A.M.—Up and at 'em.

8:00 A.M.—Phone rings. Associated Press needs another press credential.

9:00 A.M.—Arrive at office; call football office for any recent developments, such as illness, injury, changes, lineups; put press passes in order and give to ticket personnel. Phone rings constantly: "Any tickets left?" and "Will the game still be played in the rain?"

10:00 A.M.—Visiting sports information director arrives; get opponents' statistics and press guides; he or she proofs roster in game program for mistakes; take care of additional press requests.

10:30 A.M.—Student assistants and interns arrive; transport materials to press box (game programs, food, and beverages). Post additional data on the Web.

10:45 A.M.—Stop to say hello to pregame gathering of alumni.

11:00 A.M.—Get to press box; check place cards for seating arrangements; see that phones for wire services are working;

check that Internet ports and three sports information phones plugged in; check whether radio station's lines are live; go over pronunciations of players' names with visiting broadcasters (visiting SID does likewise).

11:30 A.M.—Press box crew and aides start arriving. These are: press box steward who checks passes; statisticians (three offensive, two defensive); play-by-play typist; spotters for the PA announcer; radio announcers; runners to hand out stats after each quarter; announcer; photographers (one for color, two for black-and-white on sideline); coaches' game video camera personnel. If game is being televised, recheck with production staff in truck outside stadium; most of setup is done day prior to game.

12:00 P.M.—Media start arriving; give injury update; emphasize special human-interest angle: "Our top receiver went to high school with their safety."

1:00 P.M.—Everyone set . . . countdown. Two student aides operate phone for calls from TV networks with updates on scores across country, and we give report on our game; intern gives information to announcer on records being approached or broken; announce attendance, availability of coaches for interviews after game.

4:00 P.M.—Game ends. Get ready for second mad rush; runoff stat sheets; students call in final score to television stations and other outlets; if not present, a student calls AP and UPI with 150 words on game and posts with statistics on website.

4:30 P.M.—Write and do sixty-second radio reports for local stations; give condolences to opponent SID about his or her team's loss.

5:00 P.M.—Assist the reporters with the stories that will be sent to their newspapers via Internet. Stop at postgame radio show (usually local restaurant) to provide updated statistics and obtain injury report from coach and athletic trainers.

7:00 P.M.—Return to office to send statistics for both teams to NCAA computer center for weekly compilation and release.

7:30 P.M.—Clean up and go home.

Planning Your Career as a Sports Publicist

People wishing to enter this profession must have appropriate course work in college with a major in journalism, public relations, communication arts, or a specialty in sports public relations within a sports management program. Publicists have greater opportunities to move up in the field than others in sports, as sports public relations departments expand and as individuals move up regularly. For example, Vic D'Ascenzo, former sports information director at Fairfield University, first obtained a position as a graduate assistant coach in the basketball program at Fairfield. He had served as an administrative assistant for the basketball team at Villanova University as an undergraduate English major. He then received an appointment as assistant SID at Fairfield. Later he received his master's and accepted the position as director. Currently he serves as director of fund-raising for athletics at Fairfield.

If you think you wish to gain employment at the college level, contact the College Sports Information Directors of America, the professional organization for people in this field. It provides publications, offers training sessions (workshops), organizes contests (for brochures/media), and guides and generally supports its members.

College Sports Information Directors of America
University of North Alabama
UNA-Box 5038
Florence, AL 35632
www.cosida.com

CHAPTER SIX

Sports Entrepreneurs

"Nothing is more characteristic of the genius of the American people than is their genius for athletics. Nothing is more synonymous of our national success than is our success in athletics. If I were required to indicate today that element of American life which is most indicative of our nationality, my finger would unerringly point to our athletic escutcheon."

General Douglas MacArthur
Past President, U.S. Olympic Committee

I f entrepreneurship is your thing, look no further than the numerous opportunities presenting themselves in sports and athletics. An examination of products and services available yields creativity in all sizes, shapes, and forms.

Some products have stirred controversy—baseball pitcher Curt Schilling attacked one such product and smashed one of its cameras. (He was later fined $15,000.) The attorney representing the baseball umpires stated, "It's too flawed to be used as an evaluation tool!"

The item in question is QuesTec, designed to assist umpires to adjust to the new strike zone and to become more consistent in their calls. QuesTec uses a series of cameras, computers, and confidential software to measure the flight of the ball to determine if the pitch was a strike. The umpires receive a disk following the game to evaluate themselves.

Clearly, it's an interesting idea and somewhat reminiscent of "instant replay." The QuesTec Corporation, located in Deer Park, New York, has made an impact on baseball; will it be lasting? It's too early to tell.

The entrepreneurial penchant of Americans, combined with their love of sports, yields an impressive array of business successes. Elston Howard, former New York Yankees baseball star, developed the "donut," the round piece of metal placed on the bat when batters are loosening up in the on-deck circle prior to stepping up to the plate. Elmer Van Sickle's Medi-Exercise Ball assists with exercise, development, and rehabilitation of injured players; the Strength Shoe (Strength Footwear, Metairie, Louisiana), a sneaker with a platform mounted on the bottom front, was developed to increase speed and quickness and improve vertical jump. Bill Raferty, broadcaster for ESPN, CBS, and the Sports Channel, began Bill Raferty's Broadcasting School for those wishing to break into electronic media. The litany goes on and on.

Perhaps the American entrepreneurial spirit is best exemplified by NFL Films. In 1962, Ed Sabol took a number of risks. First, he submitted a $5,000 bid to the National Football League (NFL)—double the successful bid of the previous season—for the right to film the championship game. Second, he won the right and then filmed the game differently; previously, one camera stationed in the stands high above the fifty-yard line would capture the entire game. Sabol utilized several cameras around the stadium; one filmed entirely in slow motion. The result: *Pro Football's Longest Day.* Former Commissioner Pete Rozelle's verdict: the greatest football film he had ever seen. Following a few years of adjustment, Sabol's company—NFL Films—emerged, transforming the way the world looked at professional football. Eventually the multimillion-dollar award-winning organization found itself on the cutting edge of film technology, business organization, and public relations—to the delight of fans worldwide.

As with any business enterprise, product development often takes years. Mike Hall developed the Determinator, a sophisticated pitching machine. Taking five years in development, Hall's device marries television and batting practice. A video of the pitcher (any pitcher) appears on the screen approximately fifty-five feet away, and at the appropriate moment, the ball is delivered through an opening. Hall believes his machine will revolutionize batting practice, as it closely approximates game conditions.

Hall came up with the idea for his invention following a dream. "I figure you get only one great idea in a lifetime," suggested the entrepreneur. As president of Video Baseball of America in Roswell, Georgia, he placed a machine in use at Fulton County Stadium for the Atlanta Braves. "The entire concept and idea is tremendous," stated Braves general manager Bobby Cox.

Not all sports entrepreneurs develop and manufacture a product. Some focus upon distribution. The candy bars endorsed and named for professional players quickly come to mind.

Perhaps a better example is Thera-Kinetics of Mt. Laurel, New Jersey. This organization assisted Tony Dorsett, Tim Kerr, John Elway, and other athletes and the general public with its continuous passive motion (CPM) device. This machine provides CPM to an injured or recently surgically repaired body part. Present thinking among orthopedic physicians in many cases calls for movement of the ailing limb as soon as possible following a medical procedure. Patients strapped to CPM move and exercise their limbs, and recovery time is shortened.

Jerold Zebrick, owner and president, has leased the high-tech equipment to hospitals, sports medicine rehabilitation centers, and individuals. The devices must be utilized under the supervision of a physician and the direction of a physical therapist or related health personnel. In commenting on the success of marketing his equipment to the sports world, Zebrick stated, "These guys are worth millions of dollars to their teams, and when they go down, the object is to get them back and playing as fast as possible." Fortunately for companies such as Thera-Kinetics, even most nonathletes want to return to normal activities as soon as possible following an injury.

Entrepreneurs have also found opportunities in publishing sports information. The public's hunger for sports-related news has allowed a variety of newsletters, magazines, and other publications to flourish. Some examples are:

- regional and local publications covering sports news in a given geographical area
- newsletters and magazines supporting a single university's sports teams or a professional sports franchise
- magazines and newsletters focusing on a single sport, such as wrestling or baseball

The ready availability of personal computers and desktop publishing software has made it possible for almost anyone to produce attractive, professional-looking publications. This means that if you choose to start a sports-related publication, you can get started on a small scale and then, if conditions allow, grow into a larger enterprise.

The growth of the Internet is also opening up publishing opportunities related to sports. For example, Cloverleaf Golf Publications of White Salmon, Washington, produces a series of books on golf that interested customers can download from the Internet. Newsletters and other publications can also be produced and marketed online. If you want to start your own sports publication, this is one approach. One advantage is that you can save substantially on printing and mailing costs.

Lest it seem too easy, fun, lucrative, and glamorous to own your own sports-related company, as you mingle with and interview athletes and others from the sports world, heed the words of basketball yearbook guru Mike Moriarity: "It's not that easy to make money; the business side is difficult, and competition is hell. I spend most of my time on the nonglamorous end of the business." Moriarity started out by publishing the *Big East Yearbook* on a part-time basis. The University of Missouri grad then expanded his enterprise and began publishing the *ACC Yearbook*, the *Big Ten Yearbook*, and the *Big Eight Yearbook*.

"Sports is something that appeals to everyone; friends are envious! However, if all I had to do is to watch games and edit stories, this [job] would be a blast. This is not an easy area to make money," Moriarity said.

Before starting a sports-related business, be sure to do your homework. Bookstores and libraries offer scores of books on starting and running your own business, and the local office of the U.S. Small Business Administration is a great resource (see your phone directory for the nearest office).

For a brief overview, request the publications "Starting a New Business" and "Running a Small Business." They're free on request from:

Federal Citizen Information Center
Department 71
Pueblo, CO 81009
www.pueblo.gsa.gov

Many opportunities for entrepreneurship exist. Carefully choose a special niche, work like hell, and enjoy life as a sports entrepreneur. With any luck, financial success will soon follow.

CHAPTER SEVEN

Sports Medicine Professionals

"Thanks for saving my career," said Kerry Kittles, New Jersey Nets professional basketball player to his doctor. Kittles had suffered many injuries and experienced several surgeries to his right knee. He missed one entire season because of an injury. Dr. Craig Morgan, a Delaware-based orthopedist, used a radical new procedure utilizing undamaged cartilage from one part of his knee to assist the damaged area—it worked. Kittles returned to play, contributing to his team's success.

Sports medicine professionals do marvelous things, combining the latest research, new technology, and a strong basic understanding of the human machine. They function as a team working to prevent injury, educate athletes, and restore players to normal functioning through rehabilitation.

Among this team of specialists:

- athletic trainer
- chiropractor
- dentist
- exercise physiologist
- message therapist
- nutritionist
- ophthalmologist
- optometrist
- orthopedist

- orthotist
- osteopath
- podiatrist
- physical therapist
- psychologist
- strength, fitness, and conditioning coach

David Lamb, past president of the prestigious American College of Sports Medicine, defined the field: "Sports medicine is the scientific and medical aspects of exercise and athletics." More specifically, Professor Henry Miller, M.D., of Wake Forest University in North Carolina divided sports medicine into three categories:

1. **Athletic medicine:** the evaluation, conditioning, and prevention and treatment of injuries.
2. **Research:** the physiological, biochemical, biomechanical, and behavioral aspects of athletic medicine. Includes finding new methods more successful and satisfactory than the present ones.
3. **Prevention and rehabilitation:** the treatment of chronic and degenerative disease associated with sports and athletics.

A further clarification can be obtained from the American College of Sports Medicine, which is not a college in the traditional sense but a professional society composed of more than ten thousand members. Its constitution states that the society is: "A multidisciplinary professional and scientific society dedicated to the generation and dissemination of knowledge concerning the motivation, responses, adaptation, and health of persons engaging in exercise." Specifically, the college is concerned with:

1. Basic physiological, biochemical, biomedical, and behavioral mechanisms associated with exercise.

2. Improvement and maintenance of functional capacities for daily living.
3. Prevention and rehabilitation of chronic and degenerative diseases.
4. Evaluation and conditioning of athletes.
5. Prevention and treatment of injuries related to sports and exercise.

The organization, founded in 1954, has provided guidance and knowledge to sports medicine professionals and athletes in terms of the latest athletic health procedures based upon clinical practice and serious research. The college publishes position papers as well as research and information publications, sponsors research grants, certifies certain sports medicine personnel, and conducts workshops and conferences.

The explosion of sports injuries and serious concern about permanent damage resulted in the joint proclamation by the American Medical Association and the National Federation of State High School Athletic Associations of the Athlete's Bill of Rights. Sports medicine personnel, coaches, athletes, and others should carefully examine the list, reprinted on the following pages.

Obviously, adherence to these important guidelines can serve to reduce the incidence of athletic injuries. Sports medicine personnel can make an important contribution through publicizing and orienting the athletic community to these suggestions.

Despite the apparently varied background of those involved in sports medicine, some common threads run through their backgrounds: they have a greater interest in and knowledge of science than most Americans; they have an academic orientation (most attend graduate or professional school after college); they demonstrate a human-service orientation—a willingness to help people; they attempt to add new knowledge to their profession by sharing successful clinical practices and experimental research results; they enjoy people; and they like athletics and sports.

THE ATHLETE'S BILL OF RIGHTS

Proper conditioning helps to prevent injuries by hardening the body and increasing resistance to fatigue.

1. Are the prospective players given directions and activities for preseason conditioning?
2. Is there a minimum of two weeks of practice before the game or contest?
3. Is the player required to warm up thoroughly prior to the participation?
4. Are substitutions made without hesitation when players evidence disability?

Careful coaching leads to skillful performance, which lowers the incidence of injuries.

1. Is emphasis given to safety in teaching techniques and elements of play?
2. Are injuries carefully analyzed to determine causes and suggest preventative programs?
3. Are tactics discouraged that may increase the hazards and thus the incidence of injuries?
4. Are practice periods carefully planned and of a reasonable duration?

Good officiating promotes the enjoyment of the games as well as the protection of the players.

1. Are players as well as coaches thoroughly schooled in the rules of the games?
2. Are rules and regulations strictly enforced in practice periods as well as in games?
3. Are officials employed who are qualified both emotionally and technically for their responsibilities?

The right equipment and facilities serve a unique purpose in protection of players.

1. Is the best protective equipment provided for contact sports?
2. Is careful attention given to proper fitting and adjustment of equipment?
3. Is equipment properly maintained, and are worn and outmoded items discarded?
4. Are proper areas for play provided and carefully maintained?

Adequate medical care is necessary in the prevention and control of athletic injuries.

1. Is there a thorough preseason health history and medical examination taken?
2. Is a physician present at contests and readily available during practice sessions?
3. Does the physician make the decision as to whether an athlete should return to play following injury during games?
4. Is authority from a physician required before an athlete can return to practice after being out of play because of a disabling injury?
5. Is the care given to athletes by coach or trainer limited to first aid and medically prescribed services?

Considerable opportunities for variation exist in the sports medicine career cluster. People not wishing a lengthy college commitment might consider a position as a sports physical therapy assistant, while those more academically inclined might consider the life of the sports physician or psychologist. Similarly, within the specialties, opportunities exist for several emphases.

For example, an orthopedist would have these options: working at a sports medicine center while seeing patients and conducting research, or assisting a local high school as team physician and maintaining a private practice emphasizing sports medicine.

The following sections explain the various sports medicine careers as well as providing information about general good athletic health procedures. Not only will people considering sports medicine careers find this chapter of value and interest—but coaches, athletes, and fans may also benefit.

Sports Physicians

Located at the core of the sports medicine team is the orthopedist. Orthopedists are medical doctors who perform the surgical miracles that return athletes to competition; in addition, they supervise the activities of allied health personnel. Orthopedists specialize in the health of bones and joints, related supportive structures, and muscles. Osteopathic (D.O.) and chiropractic (D.C.) specialists likewise can serve as sports physicians concentrating on their specific orientation to providing good health. Other medical specialists—for example, dentists—also may assist athletes. Regardless of the specialty of the physician, the commandments of Theodore Fox, M.D., formerly of the Chicago Bears professional football team, deserve serious attention as guidelines to behavior. These have undergone slight modification to conform to this book.

TEAM OR SPORTS PHYSICIAN'S TEN COMMANDMENTS

I. The physician must be trained in all procedures for prevention, recognition, diagnosis, and treatment of injuries; first aid; as well as knowledge of soft tissue and skeletal injuries.

2. The physician must personally examine and evaluate all candidates for the sport or team prior to their participation to determine each individual's fitness. This should include a history of all previous illnesses, accidents, and surgical procedures as well as a psychological evaluation and a thorough physical examination. The physical evaluation should include observations of any injury, especially in the collision sports. The physical examination should include determination of the individuals' maturity, balance, coordination, agility, stamina, and strength.

3. The physician must know the fundamentals of the particular sport with which he or she is involved to better understand the mechanism of the injuries occurring, as well as the injured participant and her or his problem.

4. The physician must observe and evaluate the emotional well-being of the athlete, especially the young player. Is the candidate being pushed by a frustrated parent to be a superstar or made apprehensive by a parent who is concerned that the athlete might get hurt?

5. The physician should select and fit all protective gear and equipment and check it as to type and quality, especially in the collision sports.

6. The physician should supervise the trainer or the coach in the proper use of physiotherapeutic techniques in the training room. Also, the physician is responsible for conditioning and rehabilitation exercises (such as weight training). Upon the doctor rests the responsibility for total rehabilitation of the injured athlete (mental and physical); a careful examination must precede the athlete's return to participation.

7. The physician must advise the coach not to teach dangerous blocking and checking practices and to avoid mismatches between athletes, especially young players.

The doctor should advise the coach or trainer about problems or injuries that may occur because of heat, humidity, overwork, or fatigue.

8. The physician (or a designated replacement) must be available at all times to examine injured players as soon as possible after the injury. This is especially true in collision sports where, if possible, the physician should be on field. Often youngsters will mask an injury so as to continue to play; a physician can make an assessment of the severity of the injury. Also, certain injuries (neck, re-injury) require a doctor's examination.

9. The physician must prevent an injured player from returning to the game if there exists a reasonable doubt about his or her condition. In doing so, the physician must resist all pressures from coaches, parents, alumni, and the player.

10. The doctor must obtain x-rays of injuries (and other information as necessary) prior to judging the condition of the injury.

The importance of the physician to sports may not be realized by the average fan, but the athlete recognizes the contribution. Gale Sayers, formerly an outstanding running back for the University of Kansas and the Chicago Bears, gave his opinion in his fine book *I Am Third* (Bantam): "The business of injuries to professional football players is a tricky one, with all kinds of complications. You really have to leave it up to the team doctor. I have always found Dr. Fox a man I could rely on, a man I could go to if I had problems. My philosophy about aches and pains is to get them checked out to be sure they're not going to impair your performance."

Dave Meggyesy, also a former pro football player, noted the significant role physicians play, recalling some negative experience in college *(Out of Their League;* Ramparts): "When a player is injured, he is sent to the team physician, who is usually more concerned with getting the athlete back into action than anything else. This reversal of priorities leads to unbelievable abuses."

The sports medicine staff has a serious obligation to the player's present and future health. Close adherence to Dr. Fox's Ten Commandments will curtail many of the serious abuses related to athletics.

Sports Medicine Specialties

While a few teams, mainly at schools, employ general practitioners (GPs) in the capacity of sports physicians, orthopedists, by their training, best serve in this position. Those involved in sports normally serve on a consulting basis with teams and/or work in sports clinics.

This career is the best paid of all sports medicine personnel. Yearly salaries over $150,000 are common; most earn considerably more. In addition, sports physicians enjoy fine working conditions and, in most cases, great prestige.

Many sports physicians work under the auspices of a sports medicine clinic or center. These facilities work with individual athletes and with sports teams. Often they have contracts to provide their services to local schools and colleges. Some are actually associated with colleges, such as the Temple University Center for Sports Medicine and Science in Pennsylvania; others are privately owned and operated, such as the Stone Clinic in San Francisco, California. Typical functions of a sports clinic include:

- diagnosis and treatment of acute athletic injuries
- rehabilitation of athletic injuries
- referral resource for team and family physicians
- preventative education

A clinic or center's staff is made up of a team of sports medicine professionals: orthopedists, athletic trainers, physical therapists, and other specialists on a consulting basis as needed, such as dentists or nutritionists. Most centers have the latest and finest equipment, both diagnostic and rehabilitative. These centers frequently serve nonathletes who wish to avail themselves of the latest aggressive prevention, diagnostic, and rehabilitation procedures and, if required, surgery. The medical aspects of the center fall under the jurisdiction of the orthopedist.

Orthopedics. Orthopedists attend undergraduate college and then enter medical school. After graduation, they concentrate on their chosen field. This involves more course work, individual study, and practical experience. The internship takes one year, and the residency normally four years, so the total education of the orthopedist involves nine years after college! During the residency period, the young doctor works under the supervision of an experienced orthopedic physician, conducting examinations, directing first aid, performing surgery, and designing rehabilitation programs. Not all orthopedists go into sports medicine; some set up private practice and work to correct deformities related mainly to muscle, joint, and bone problems. If a person has a serious accident requiring surgery, such as cartilage damage to a knee or a hip replacement, an orthopedist would be involved. Most have very specific subspecialties and focus upon surgical procedures relative to the ankle, hip, or knee joints. With increased attention to sports injury prevention and rehabilitation, opportunities for careers as a doctor with a specialty in orthopedics will continue to be very good.

Additional information concerning medical doctors (M.D.s) may be obtained from the following:

American College of Sports Medicine
P.O. Box 1440
Indianapolis, IN 46206
www.acsm.org

American Medical Association
515 North State Street
Chicago, IL 60610
www.ama-assn.org

American Orthopaedic Society for Sports Medicine
6300 North River Road, Suite 500
Rosemont, IL 60018
www.sportsmed.org

Association of American Medical Colleges
2450 North Street NW
Washington, DC 20037
www.aamc.org

Bookmarking this wonderful website is strongly suggested: *The Physician and Sports Medicine* at www.physsportsmed.com.

Osteopathic Medicine. Osteopathic Physicians (D.O.s), like medical doctors, utilize surgery, drugs, and other acceptable health care practices. In addition, they may use manipulation (treatment using the hands or mechanical means) and emphasize the treatment of the whole athlete in designing a conditioning or rehabilitation program.

While still not totally accepted by some medical doctors, osteopathic medicine has made great gains in recent years. In Detroit, all four professional sports teams utilize osteopaths as their team physicians. The educational requirements of osteopathic colleges almost parallel those of medical colleges, and osteopaths wishing to specialize likewise complete a rigorous residency. However, they are not certified medical doctors.

Salaries of osteopaths lag behind those of medical doctors. However, most do well—$50,000 to $100,000 a year or more—and those in sports medicine do even better. Opportunities for employment for osteopaths in the future will continue to remain very good as sports medicine expands and the public comes to further respect the work of doctors of osteopathic medicine.

As with medical doctors, osteopaths undertake residencies upon graduation from osteopathic college; for those interested in sports medicine, the residency takes from three to five years. Regardless of specialty, all D.O.s must obtain licensing in all states.

For those interested in sports medicine, osteopathy deserves serious consideration. For more information, contact:

American Osteopathic Association
142 East Ontario Street
Chicago, IL 60611
www.aoa-net.org

Chiropractic Medicine. Chiropractic physicians (D.C.s) emphasize the use of manipulation as their primary treatment. They believe that a person's (in this case the athlete's) health, to a large degree, relates to the welfare of the nervous system. Interference with the system thus impairs normal function and lowers resistance to disease. Chiropractors generally work with the spine to restore proper functioning to the nervous system. In addition to manipulation, they use water, light, massage, ultrasound, electric, and heat therapy. Often they prescribe a special diet, nutritional supplements, exercise, and rest to heal the injured athlete. They do not believe in using prescription drugs or surgery as part of their approach, nor are they permitted by the state in which they practice to do this, because they are not medical doctors.

More than thirty thousand licensed chiropractors practice the profession in the United States. Most have private offices, while others work at clinics and chiropractic colleges where they engage in teaching and/or research. Those engaged in sports medicine usually make it known that they specialize in the treatment of athletes. Some teams maintain a chiropractor as a consultant, should they need such services.

A strong interest in sports medicine exists among chiropractors. In addition, some former athletes have entered the profession. For example, Dr. Fred Cox, former placekicker for the Minnesota Vikings professional football team, went on to become a chiropractor.

The expansion and acceptance of chiropractic medicine will result in continued improvements in salaries, which currently lag behind those of physicians but may exceed $80,000 per year.

If this profession interests you, contact:

American Chiropractic Association
1701 Clarendon Boulevard
Arlington, VA 22209
www.amerchiro.org

International Chiropractors Association
1110 North Glebe Road, Suite 1000
Arlington, VA 22201
www.chiropractic.org

Council on Chiropractic Education
7975 North Eighty-Fifth Way
Scottsdale, AZ 85258
www.cce-usa.org

....

Athletic Trainers

"Training athletes is the greatest profession in the world for helping people," said Michael O'Shea, M.A., ATC, University of Louisville. "The athlete trainer is a twenty-four-hour father confessor to all, both men and women, young and old. I take great pride in being an athletic trainer and a part of the NATA."

Athletic trainers receive a specific education to serve in the sports world and are unique sports medicine personnel in that regard. Consequently, they often have considerable importance and influence over the direction of sports medicine at their institutions and in general.

An athletic trainer's duties consist of the implementation of an injury-prevention program and the initiation of immediate treatment and rehabilitation procedures for the injured athlete as directed by the team physician. He or she is the person you see down on the field or sitting on the bench close to the large first-aid kit. Long before the contest, the trainer has prepared the participants, taping some and providing therapy for others. He or she stays after the game, providing services as needed.

Telephone calls come in on the deposition of x-rays taken of an injured athlete, coaches call to make requests about certain safety equipment newly available, and parents call to ask about an injury their child suffered; similar other requests regularly arrive. It's not a career for someone looking for an easy job. Specifically, trainers engage in the following activities:

- Selecting proper equipment in cooperation with the coaching staff and the equipment manager. In this regard, new developments—such as those in pediatrics or dentistry—should be reported to the coaching staff.
- Supervising safety factors involving playing areas—that is, the removal of items players may run into and the repair of equipment constituting a safety hazard.
- Assisting in the application of injury-preventive devices, such as helping and assisting with braces and similar gear and reminding athletes to utilize such equipment if necessary.
- Planning a conditioning and injury-prevention program with the coaching staff and other sports medicine personnel.
- Maintaining the athletic training area and its equipment, including ordering supplies, supervising the servicing of equipment, and keeping careful health records.

- Administering first aid to injured athletes. This would involve both minor problems, like a sprained ankle, and major difficulties requiring transporting the player to a hospital.
- Developing and supervising a rehabilitation program under the supervision of a physician. This duty would include monitoring the use of exercises shown to the athlete, and it may involve the utilization of ultrasound or the whirlpool.
- Reporting to the coach and physician the rehabilitation progress of the athlete. This involves the gain of strength in the affected area as measured by technical equipment. This is one of the most important tasks of the trainer, as it involves determining how soon the injured player may return to action.
- Serving as an executive and educator. As an administrator, the trainer maintains a budget, develops a student trainers program, and supervises the student trainers. In a major athletic program, there is a head trainer, and he or she has a staff of assistant athletic trainers.
- Establishing and maintaining good interpersonal relationships with the coaching staff, the sports medicine consultants, and the players. The trainer serves as the head of the control center.

The importance of proper conditioning involving strength, cardiovascular fitness, and flexibility cannot be overemphasized. The list on the following page contains the Ten Cardinal Principles of Athletic Conditioning that every coach, player, and sports medicine professional must know and implement. The specific accountability rests with the athletic trainer.

Obviously, the duties and obligations are significant, and the athletic trainer's importance to sports continues to increase. Otho Davis, trainer emeritus for the Philadelphia Eagles and former executive director of the National Athletic Trainers Association,

TEN CARDINAL PRINCIPLES OF ATHLETIC CONDITIONING

1. **Warm-up.** Each activity must be preceded by an adequate warm-up. Stretching activities and running will provide the greatest benefit following a mild warm-up. Warming down (includes stretching again) likewise requires attention.
2. **Gradualness.** Start slowly to condition someone and look to peak at a certain time. Setting goals can be helpful.
3. **Timing.** Athletes must be counseled not to overdo workouts; relaxation and rest form part of every conditioning program.
4. **Intensity.** Workouts and practices must be characterized by quality and continuous activity with appropriate rest periods.
5. **Capacity level.** While cautious to avoid the above pitfalls, athletes will want to work to capacity and should be encouraged to do so.
6. **Strength.** Greater endurance, speed, flexibility, and confidence will result from improved strength.
7. **Motivation.** Sports medicine personnel can reinforce the coaches' techniques to stimulate players.
8. **Specialization.** Include exercises in each player's conditioning program to improve the player in relation to the sport he or she wishes to play and her or his weakness.
9. **Relaxation.** Trainers should familiarize themselves with specific techniques to teach players how to relax and thereby recover from tension, fatigue, and stress.
10. **Routine.** A planned daily, weekly, and monthly routine must be constructed for each player in cooperation with the athlete and coach.

believes that the most important role of the trainer is to prevent an injury from occurring because at the professional level a player cannot afford to miss practice. For the Eagles, conditioning occurs eleven-plus months a year. After a short break following the season, many players begin a new program. Two days each week, running for cardiovascular endurance and agility is emphasized. Three days focus on weight training. Specific training to improve a weakness likewise occurs.

Many athletic trainers have management responsibilities. Serving in this role in a large university may involve supervising assistant trainers and other staff. It may also involve administering departmental budgets.

One of the most visible (via television) trainers is Ronnie Barnes. He serves as head athletic trainer for the New York Giants and is active in the National Association of Athletic Trainers. Barnes said, "If you're not good enough to play, yet still want to be in on the sports action down on the field or on the court, seriously consider the position of athletic trainer." Barnes served as athletic trainer at East Carolina University, where he received his bachelor's degree, and at Michigan State University, from which he obtained his master's degree before undertaking his present position. He also earned the Athletic Trainer Certificate (ATC).

Serving as an athletic trainer for the Giants may sound glamorous, and it is! "The profession demands hard work, long hours, and travel, but it's exciting," Barnes said. "The profession is still in its infancy—I particularly enjoy the breakthroughs in terms of new ways to improve athletic performance, such as a new stretching program or weight-training regimen."

Despite the entry of large numbers into this profession, job prospects continue to look good. A number of high schools have added athletic trainers to their staffs. In 1985 North Carolina became the first state to require them for high schools, and this trend has spread. For example, Orange County, Florida, instituted a similar mandate in 1990. Andrew Clary, University of Miami head athletic trainer, noted that "the future in this job is tremendous, not only in school settings but in corporate fitness." Clary believes his profession makes a unique contribution to sports medicine because of its practitioners' unique knowledge of soft tissue (muscle). The undergraduate athletic training option at Penn State University typifies most programs. It includes the following courses:

- Orientation to Athletic Training
- Advanced Athletic Training
- Recognition and Physical Examination of Athletic Injury
- Foundation of Therapeutic Exercise
- Exercise Physiology
- Introduction to Therapeutic Modalities
- Administrative Aspects of Athletic Training

Additional related courses and other university requirements round out the program.

While disappointed with the general level of salaries, Barnes stated, "Athletic training is still an up-and-coming profession. It is particularly wide open for minorities who have entered this career only in small numbers."

The major trainers organization, the National Athletic Trainers Association (NATA), certifies trainers, who receive the Athletic Trainer Certificate. NATA also evaluates college athletic training programs. For information, contact:

National Athletic Trainers Association (NATA)
2952 Stemmons Freeway, Suite 200
Dallas, TX 75247
www.nata.org

NATA's *Journal of Athletic Training* contains professional information as well as articles by sports medicine personnel.

Another organization of interest is the National Strength and Conditioning Association. This group, through its publications and website, provides valuable information to athletes, coaches, personal trainers, medical personnel, and others in the sports community.

National Strength and Conditioning Association
P.O. Box 9908
Colorado Springs, CO 80932
www.nsca-lift.org

Canadian Kinesiology Alliance
6519-B Mississauga Road
Mississauga, ON L5N 1A6
Canada
www.cka.ca

Sports Physical Therapist

Sports physical therapists work with athletes who have been disabled through accident, birth defect, or illness. Some therapists work with athletes sent to them by a physician to aid in the rehabilitation of an injury. Treatments include:

- exercises for increasing strength, endurance, coordination, and range of motion
- activities to facilitate motor capacity or learning
- instruction in activities of daily living and use of assistance devices
- application of physical agents such as heat and cold, sound, water, and acupuncture to relieve pain and/or alter physiological status

Physical therapists attend college to receive certification in their profession; some attend graduate programs and enter leadership positions in the field. Certification requires pursuing certain course work and, in forty-nine of fifty states, passing an examination to receive a license to treat patients.

A typical college program includes courses in the basics of physical therapy, physical agents, patient evaluation and treatment, and therapeutic exercise, as well as in medical areas such as pharmacology and pathology. Students also pursue a regular complement of courses required by the college. In addition to their professional area courses and electives, they may wish to take work in sports studies and sciences, such as athletic training.

Many physical therapists who work with athletes do so at sports medicine clinics, where they assist other professionals in rehabilitating athletes. This team approach undoubtedly will continue to characterize the profession for the future.

Salaries, typically in the $50,000 to $90,000 range, will continue to increase as the sports profession and the public come to realize the value of physical therapy.

If you wish additional information, read *Opportunities in Physical Therapy Careers* by Bernice R. Krumhansl and Kathy Siebel (VGM Career Books) or contact:

American Academy of Physical Medicine and Rehabilitation
One IBM Plaza, Suite 2500
Chicago, IL 60611
www.aapmr.org

American Academy of Physical Therapy
CB 19412
Winston Salem, NC 27110
www.aaptnet.org

American Physical Therapy Association
1111 North Fairfax Street
Alexandria, VA 22314
www.apta.org

Canadian Physiotherapy Association
2345 Yonge Street, Suite 410
Toronto, ON M4P 2E5
Canada
www.physiotherapy.ca

Other Sports Medicine Professionals

The fabulous growth of sports medicine has touched every area of the medical and allied professions. Specialists applying their unique skills and knowledge to improve athletic performance include dentists, vision specialists such as optometrists and ophthalmologists, exercise physiologists, psychologists, massage therapists, nutritionists, podiatrists, orthotists and prosthetists, and others.

Sports Dentists

Hank Iervolino, former baseball pitcher for New York Technological University, once said: "When I've tried pitching without the mouthguard, I get tired quicker and feel more pain in my arm afterwards. Some might say it's psychological, but I don't think so."

One of the areas of sports medicine that has created excitement in recent decades has been the use of special mouthpieces. Interest in these devices skyrocketed following a 1980s *Sports Illustrated* report. Technically called a mandibular orthopedic repositioning application (MORA), this dental apparatus fits over the lower teeth and readjusts the misalignment from which some athletes suffer. The players reported increased overall performance and particularly improved strength. Dr. Richard Kaufman, a Long Island, New York, orthodontist and a pioneer in this field, noted, "It is essential to place the jaw in a proper position to enable the athlete to function at his maximum potential capacity. I have been conducting tests to show that injuries can be reduced and overall physical functioning can be increased by using a custom-fitted mouthpiece which places the jaw in optimum position."

While not all research agrees with Kaufman, there is general agreement that the position of the jaw has much to do with total body energy and muscle strength. Additional research is presently being conducted to validate the effectiveness of the MORA. Undoubtedly, for some individuals, this device will have a beneficial effect. For a dentist with an interest in sports, the ongoing development of special mouth devices makes this a very exciting career.

Most sports dentists serve athletes in many traditional ways. They work with players to help them avoid injury to the mouth area through the use of dental devices, if necessary, and other protection, such as mouth and face guards in football and mouth guards in field hockey. The utilization of the mouthpiece and face guard has cut injuries by 60 percent. In addition, the dentists provide regular oral examinations; nothing will "bench" an athlete faster than an abscessed tooth. In the case of injury to the mouth, the dentist provides appropriate treatment.

Few, if any, dentists involve themselves with sports on a full-time basis. In addition to their regular practices, some dentists serve athletic teams as consultants. They are paid a yearly fee for their duties relating to the team. Others volunteer their services to school and community teams.

The American Dental Association (ADA) has outlined the general primary functions of the team dentist:

1. The dentist is responsible for making sure that players have good oral health at the start of the season.
2. The team dentist helps set up and implement the school mouth protector program. Each year, the dentist and school officials should discuss when the program should take place, how and by whom it will be run, what kind of protectors should be used, and what the cost will be.

3. The team dentist can treat emergency dental problems if the player's own dentist is not available, or can administer first aid if the team physician is not present.

The ADA provides additional suggestions, guidelines, and information to dentists to assist them in this highly specialized area.

The Committee on Dental Health, part of the U.S. Olympic Committee's Sports Medicine Council, serves athletes and athletics in four ways. First, it serves in an educational fashion by helping athletes realize that total health includes "dental fitness." For example, a requirement was implemented that women participating in field hockey must wear a mouthpiece when playing under the auspices of the U.S. Olympic Committee. Committee members hope that this requirement will have an educational effect by trickling down to the college and high school level.

Second, the Committee on Dental Health screens athletes prior to international competition. In some cases, the treatment of an infected tooth has resulted in dramatic improvement in the athlete's performance. The committee not only works with athletes, but has also serviced fans at the Olympic Games.

Third, the committee provides remedial care and assists in securing dental care in or near the athlete's hometown. For example, the committee prepared a national list of dentists with an interest in and appropriate skills for working with athletes.

Fourth, the committee fosters research, such as the experiments conducted on the value of the MORA.

Dental care should be part of the total training program of every athlete and every athletic team. Fortunately, coaches and players have realized this; in the future, many opportunities will exist for the dentist interested in sports medicine.

The education of a dentist is a long, arduous process. It requires excellent academic performance in high school, college, and professional dental school. However, the rewards are great. Sports dentistry can provide the opportunity to work with athletes on an ongoing basis and the chance to invent and develop dental devices contributing to increased athletic performance.

Additional information about dentistry can be found in the book *Opportunities in Dental Care* by Bonnie Kendall (VGM Career Books) and from:

American Dental Association
211 East Chicago Avenue
Chicago, IL 60611
www.ada.org

Sports Vision Specialists

From Seiderman's and Schneider's *The Athletic Eye:* "It used to be that athletes would go to the eye doctor, read the chart, and either be given a prescription for glasses or be sent home. That was then. Today there are options."

Historically, most individuals and athletes have been measured for their static visual acuity (SVA)—how well they could read a stationary eye chart while seated. However, athletes don't function in their sport in this fashion. Enter dynamic visual acuity (DVA)—how well moving players see moving objects. Today's sports vision specialists emphasize the importance of visual acuity to athletic success and introduce techniques to enhance such skills, particularly DVA.

Bausch and Lomb's Council on Sports Vision has discovered these early warning signs for detection of vision problems:

- athletes who squint to see clearly
- football players who have difficulty seeing the ball and catching passes
- tennis players who have difficulty focusing on the ball and reacting to the serve
- golfers who have trouble discerning the distance to the green

- basketball players who are uncertain in their ball handling, miss too many free throws, or tend to close one eye when they shoot
- athletes who constantly rub their eyes or suffer from headaches or excessive tearing

While most of the public, including athletes, remain unaware of the dynamic value of vision, Steven and Greggory DeVore have had excellent results working with a variety of athletes. Results of the DeVore brothers' technique have included the following:

- At California State University at Hayward, two of the lowest-ranking tennis players tried the technique. The results made international news. Their coach commented, "In all my years of coaching, I have never seen such rapid progress in athletes before."
- Doug True, who played on the University of California basketball team, utilized the system to improve his shooting percentage. He later was drafted by the Phoenix Suns of the National Basketball Association.

This training system has the potential to attract more and more athletes, and additional sports optometrists (and optometric assistants and technicians) may be necessary to implement this program or others of its type.

For people thinking of a career in a sports-related profession, one of the most exciting and rewarding will be in sports vision. Dr. Burt Fisher, who has assisted members of the Dallas Cowboys and other teams, lamented, "It seems odd that parents and coaches will spend so much time developing a young athlete and so much money purchasing the necessary equipment and padding and then ignore proper eye care." Fortunately, the message of Dr. Fisher and his fellow sports vision specialists has begun to attract attention; future players in all sports at all levels will give serious attention to this aspect of human performance.

As with other medical personnel, the education and training of ophthalmologists (M.D.s) and optometrists (D.O.s) requires a serious commitment and long study. One important criterion for success is an interest in science and academics. Opportunities also exist for paraprofessionals to serve in this area as technicians and assistants. Normally these require shorter training periods, such as in a trade school or community college. Salaries are considerably below that of eye doctors.

For additional information, consult the book *Opportunities in Eye Care Careers* by Kathleen M. Beilkoff (VGM Career Books) or contact the professional organization of optometrists at the following address:

American Optometric Association
243 North Lindbergh Boulevard
St. Louis, MO 63141
www.aoanet.org

Exercise Physiologists

Breakthroughs in physical training and fitness conditioning occur continuously. Despite a string of broken records and superior athletic successes, additional information needs to be discovered. Heading the movement to maximize athletic performance are exercise physiologists. Those involved in athletics normally work at sports centers, some located on college campuses, and perform the following major functions:

- assisting serious and weekend athletes to achieve fitness
- developing team conditioning and injury-prevention programs with coaches and other sports medicine personnel
- evaluating the potential of athletes
- helping players to recover from injury
- working with world-class athletes to improve their performances

The underlying assumption of exercise physiologists (who most often work closely with a variety of other sports medicine professionals) is that through analysis of the elements of athletic prowess, they will be able to teach athletes to perform even better. Consequently, across the nation and the world, new research continues to provide innovative methods of evaluating performance and training techniques.

One area of major contribution has come in the realm of women's athletics. Just a couple of decades ago, sports and athletics generally were believed to be too demanding and too intense for most women. Fortunately, the myth that women cannot engage in conditioning and training activities has largely disappeared. Professor George Colfer of Texas A&M University reviewed the research on women and physical activity and developed the following conclusions:

1. Women can be athletically skilled and rigorously trained.
2. Women are perfectly capable of performing strenuous activities without any physical impairment.
3. Active women possess a better state of health than those who are inactive.
4. Women are capable of high-level motor tasks as well as those involving endurance capabilities.
5. Strength can be developed or improved in women at a higher ratio than that of men.

Colfer concluded that the training needs of women are basically the same as those for men, and there is no reason to invent different training techniques for women.

Jill White is typical of the people entering the exercise physiology profession. An athlete in basketball and track at Brittenkill High School in New York, she completed her undergraduate degree at Ithaca College, then enrolled in the exercise physiology program at the University of Delaware, where she earned a master's degree. She then pursued additional graduate studies at the University of Georgia for her doctorate. Presently she is a tenured professor at Emory University in Atlanta. Dr. White's special expertise and research interests lie in sports medicine. She is living her dream. "I was always very interested in athletics (my father was a college coach) and science, and when I found out you could study sports science, I was ecstatic," said White.

Exercise physiologists utilize modern technology to complete their tasks. Slow-motion films, videotapes, and computers give clues for perfecting performance. For example, by using a biomechanical computer analyzing the placement of the joints of the body, scientists have discovered that keeping the feet flat against the ground throughout the entire throwing motion will yield the greatest distance for the javelin thrower.

In analyzing performance, Dr. Marvin Clein, founder and director of the University of Denver Human Performance Laboratory, explained some of his procedures: "The first thing you look at when you test an athlete is the ability to use oxygen." Clein said that the physical capacity to deliver powerful explosive force (arm power or leg power) serves as an important prerequisite. The laboratory looks at other aspects of the athlete's physiology. For example, bowed legs can assist football running backs; fast-twitch muscle fibers react well to quick-moving, high-intensity sports; narrow hips enable long-distance runners to amass medals.

Following the receipt of her doctorate at the University of Miami, Pat Mosher put her knowledge of exercise physiology to good use. She joined the faculty at the University of Tennessee at Chattanooga as director of the school's Human Performance Laboratory.

"This is a great career for people-oriented persons who enjoy helping their fellow human beings, and it never gets tedious," noted Dr. Mosher. "I love what I'm doing and I'm very enthusiastic about seeing people improve." She had the experience of working and conducting research at the University of Miami's Human

Performance Laboratory while earning her master's and doctorate. Dr. Mosher recommended that in addition to a strong background in science, course work in physical education and computers will prove beneficial.

The career of exercise physiology remains wide open for people who are interested in the sports aspects of the work of exercise physiologists. The preparation requires the completion of a master's degree (M.S.); many students also complete the doctorate (Ph.D.). Frequently, exercise physiologists with master's degrees gain employment in corporate fitness centers or sports medicine centers.

Many universities with an interest in sports medicine prepare exercise physiologists through interdisciplinary course work with a strong science emphasis. For additional program information, write to the colleges of your choice; address your letter to the attention of the director, Exercise Physiology Program.

Sports Psychologists

The game of sport has changed—now the athlete must be in great shape not only physically, but also mentally. For some, this involves the use of sports psychologists.

One of the fastest-growing and most interesting of careers is that of sports psychologist. These individuals utilize the methods and techniques of psychology and related fields to maximize athletic performance and well-being. Essentially, they help the athlete gain a competitive edge over rivals.

The cases from the files of Henry R. Reiter, a Long Island, New York, sports psychologist with success in working with a variety of athletes in tennis, golf, boxing, swimming, and professional baseball, are typical.

One of his clients was a fourteen-year-old, semisuccessful female tennis player. Although intelligent, she unfortunately had a terrible temper and following a mistake would throw a tantrum. Her great potential was not being realized—frequently she came close but never won a major tournament. A program was set up to work with her and her parents over a six-month period. It included some hypnosis and self-hypnosis, relaxation therapy, and the rule that the parents did not attend tournaments. The therapy was designed to help lower the player's tension level and help her gain better control over her emotions. One technique dictated that following a mistake, she would silently count—three, two, one—and then yell, "Next point!" She began to win and went on to become a successful collegiate tennis player at a California college.

A professional golfer on the pro tour had difficulty with concentration. At this point in his career, he was earning enough to cover his expenses. However, with some training on concentration, he became a more successful golfer, in both skill and income. Dr. Reiter explained that "this was an easy case; sports psychologists have had excellent results assisting in improving athletes' concentration."

A professional baseball pitcher became a client of Dr. Reiter, who noted, "He had no self-confidence—I mean zero—and he was slightly paranoid." During a period of five months, meeting twice a week, the use of hypnotherapy and hypnosis helped the pitcher develop confidence. He asked to be traded to begin anew in a different environment. He was traded, and he has become very successful.

Most sports psychologists entering the profession today have master's and usually doctoral degrees. In the past, people with backgrounds in athletic training, exercise physiology, and physical education might have functioned as sports counselors. However, the advent of malpractice lawsuits has quickly changed this situation. Those lacking appropriate degrees in psychology and counseling will be unable to obtain necessary malpractice insurance.

The doctoral degree requires both intelligence and persistence. When in a college program, take additional courses in the social or behavioral sciences with a major in psychology, and take sports studies or physical education courses when possible. While some universities have specific doctoral programs in sports psychology, most students wishing to enter this profession attend doctoral programs in clinical psychology. Within such programs, they apply the psychological concepts and theories to sports and athletics and, most importantly, undertake their training in clinic work with sports clients, utilizing psychological applications in their work. The latter is done under supervision; the doctoral dissertation would focus upon sports psychology. Several master's level programs exist for students not wishing to pursue doctoral studies.

Sports psychologists operate in a number of settings—as consultants to teams, as college professors, and as private practitioners maintaining an office practice. It is not unusual to find many serving on a college faculty and on a part-time basis working with teams or individuals. Salaries for these individuals range from $50,000 to $100,000 or more. The pace often runs hectic, but most sports psychologists enjoy the combination of academic (college) and practical (working with clients).

Team psychologists most often gain employment with a professional team on a contract basis. They work on specific goals with the team, collectively and individually, and are available if needed in a time of crisis. They may handle such individual problems as substance addiction or loss of confidence as well as team difficulties, including surviving a losing streak and coping with an irrationality, like an opponent with a "jinx" over them.

It's an enjoyable lifestyle that also can be financially rewarding. Dr. Reiter commented that "one of the joys of this job is to see one of my clients reach their potential and enjoy doing it. Another reason I like my job is I really enjoy the variety of people with whom I work."

Bob Rotella of the University of Virginia succinctly summarized the dominant feelings toward this field: "Many athletes and coaches find a fuller understanding of the role of the mind and emotions most helpful in enhancing performance."

This appreciation of the value of this young field has come because many athletes benefit from the profession's methods.

Julie K. Anthony formerly served on the staff of the Philadelphia Flyers hockey team. She taught relaxation exercises to some of the players: "The player sits in a relaxed position and progressively tenses and relaxes all the major muscles in the body." The players practice this twice a day for fifteen minutes; eventually they get to the point where, with a few deep breaths, they can tense and relax to finally relax the entire body. Anthony explained its value: "In the game, if the score is close and he is waiting to go in, an athlete can use this technique to prevent getting too tight."

Another technique of the profession—hypnosis—has aided several athletes. Bill Buckner, a former first baseman who was a fine hitter with several major league baseball clubs, hit a serious batting slump at one point during his career. "When things are going wrong, sometimes it's hard to analyze it," Buckner said. "Under hypnosis, I was better able to talk about my batting motion and what I was doing wrong. Then, when I was still hypnotized, my doctor reminded me of the things I should be working on." Buckner experienced excellent success following his counseling.

Most recently, the technique of "imagery," or "fantasy," has received a lot of attention. Recent research has shown that once athletes advance beyond the beginner stage, mental rehearsal combined with the physical practice, as opposed to practice alone, is more effective in preparing for an event. Steve Hebb, as a member of the U.S. Alpine Ski Team, used to sit and mentally visualize himself making his run: "I see myself making a perfect turn in the toughest part of the course." Dr. Richard M. Swinn of Colorado State University said that "this technique can be beneficial in ridding the athlete of negative [thinking patterns]."

Sports psychology is booming as amateur and professional athletes begin to realize its value and begin to take advantage of these modern techniques. In addition, weekend athletes wanting to improve their golf game or jump shot are availing themselves of these strategies. While few full-time positions have developed, opportunities seem promising. The success in conditioning the minds of athletes promises continued growth of the sports psychology profession. For additional information, contact:

American Board of Sports Psychology
675 Academy 2E
New York, NY 10034
www.americanboardofsportspsychology.org

The Journal of Applied Psychology
P.O. Box 1897
Lawrence, KS 66044
www.apa.org/journals/apl.htm

North American Society for the Psychology of Sport and
    Physical Activity (NASPSPA)
Department of Health and Kinesiology
Texas A&M University
MS 4243
College Station, TX 77843
www.naspspa.org

Sports Massage Therapist

Professional, amateur, and weekend athletes, in their continuing desire to prepare their minds and bodies for the test of competition, have discovered sports massage therapy.

Howard "Dr. Bucky" Grace of Westtown, Pennsylvania, observed that "those athletes who avail themselves of massage seem to derive a greater benefit than their less-athletic counterparts." Grace focuses his energies and his "magic" hands on the entire body, then gives special attention to the part of the body relative to the athlete's sport. For example, runners get extra treatment for their legs; many athletes indicate to the therapist areas of extra emphasis.

Neal Sherman, an Illinois massage therapist, commented, "I combine a judicious combination of Swedish massage and rolfing.

A lot depends upon the athlete's personality, game, and the injury history of the athlete." Some athletes prefer the laying on of the hands prior to an event or practice to prepare for the competition, while others prefer a massage afterward to facilitate recovery.

Some teams employ massage practitioners to work with their players to promote circulation, alleviate stress, and aid overall well-being. The University of Florida's women's tennis and gymnastics teams and the National Hockey League's New Jersey Devils have utilized such services.

The education requirements for massage practitioners vary according to individual states. Many states do not require certification. However, there exists a growing movement from all massage specialists to have taken training from appropriate schools, and to have those institutions be properly accredited. Check to see if the school you wish to attend has the required certification. Also many philosophies and practices of massage exist. You should be compatible with the school's orientation. As an example, examine the website of the Pennsylvania School of Muscle Therapy (www.psmt.com); you will be amazed not only with its accredited courses, but also with the variety of advanced courses, such as Professional Reflexology, Message Therapy for Cancer Patients and the Seriously Ill, and Newborn Massage. To request a catalogue, write to:

Pennsylvania School of Muscle Therapy
P.O. Box 400
Oaks, PA 19456
www.psmt.com

The following organizations can help you locate a program:

American Massage Therapy Association
820 Davis Street, Suite 100
Evanston, IL 60201
www.amtamassage.org

Associated Bodywork and Massage Professionals
1271 Sugarbush Drive
Evergreen, CO 80439
www.abmp.com

Sports Nutritionists

For centuries, people engaged in athletics looked for "the edge"—something that would enable them to produce an excellent, competitive performance. This pursuit usually centered on conditioning and stamina, and more recently on weight training, stretching, and mental toughness.

The rapid major advances in nutrition and the growing awareness of them by the public, the medical establishment, and the sports establishment will catapult sports nutritionists into a major role in the years ahead.

Most nutritionists involved in sports serve in a consultation capacity with coaches, teams, and individual athletes. They offer suggestions regarding weight control, pregame meals, and vitamin and mineral supplementation. They usually are associated with a sports medicine center, a clinic, or a college.

Professional sports nutritionists may have backgrounds and education in either medicine or nutrition. Some also may have obtained their training as dieticians, nurses, athletic trainers, and physical therapists. Through additional study and reading, the latter individuals have prepared themselves to serve the sports community as nutritionists. For example, Jim Corea, a physical therapist, undertook additional college studies in nutrition in graduate school. He used the background in developing a Philadelphia radio program as well as in his daily practice.

One individual in this field, Dr. Sarah Short, a professor of nutrition at Syracuse University, developed an interest in computerized sports nutrition. Dr. Short has investigated the nutrition requirements of various athletes (football players, wrestlers, swimmers, and others) in terms of protein, calories, minerals, vitamins, and other nutrients. The increase of such attention to sports nutrition may encourage allied health personnel to gravitate to the field of nutrition.

Michael Colgan, director of the Colgan Institute in Encinitas, California, has studied the impact of nutrition on athletes, provides nutritional information, and writes regularly on fitness and nutrition. The Colgan Institute has received contracts to investigate the value of diet and mineral, vitamin, or herbal supplementation on conditioning, strength, and performance of athletes.

Another nutritionist, Dr. Ann Grandsean, founded the International Center for Sports Nutrition in Omaha, Nebraska. "The center encourages scientific research and provides information to athletes and physically active people interested in the benefits of good nutrition," Dr. Grandsean explained. She has also served as the chief nutritional consultant to the U.S. Olympic Committee and to the University of Nebraska athletic department; in addition, she has worked with the Chicago White Sox. Dr. Grandsean said, "There is a genuine need to rapidly translate the most current research findings into easy-to-understand, useful, and factual information for athletes, coaches, and others involved in the training of our amateur athletes."

Some schools offer medical degrees (M.D.s) with a specialty in nutrition, and many additional graduate schools provide doctorates (Ph.D.s). For those not wishing advanced study, some schools of allied health science offer bachelor's degrees in nutrition.

Some enter this field with degrees in physical education, dietary science, chiropractic science, or nursing. This may provide an initial background, but considerable additional study must be undertaken to understand the complex biochemical needs of the body. Some individuals with training in naturopathic or holistic medicine do well in this field. For more information, contact:

National Association of Sports Nutrition
7710 Balboa, Suite 227B
San Diego, CA 92111
www.nasnutrition.com

The International Center for Sports Nutrition
502 South Forty-Fourth Street, Suite 3012
Omaha, NE 68105

Sports Podiatrists

It's a rare sport that does not put great strain on the participant's feet. For the estimated 80 percent of all people who have foot problems, even minor ones, the increase of physical activity can worsen these situations.

These difficulties normally lead the injured party to the office of a podiatrist. These health professionals, usually identified by the initials D.P.M. (doctor of podiatric medicine), specialize in foot care. Utilizing medical, surgical, and physical techniques, they work to prevent or treat foot injuries and diseases.

Dr. Lee Cohen of Morton, Pennsylvania, developed a Cushioned Anti-Pronation Insert (CAPI) for athletes. The device serves as a shock absorber and is part of Dr. Cohen's preventative approach to sports medicine. He stated, "It's no fun to see forty or fifty people a day complaining of pain. It's more efficient to take some preventative steps ahead of time." Dr. Cohen further said that "we need to make the change from sports medicine to sports-injury prevention."

Additional information about this profession may be obtained from:

American Academy of Podiatric Sports Medicine
1729 Glastonberry Road
Potomac, MD 20854
www.aapsm.org

Sports Orthotists and Prosthetists

Following several elbow problems with players, the New York Islanders hockey team contacted Andy Myers, a specialist in orthotics and prosthetics. He designed a brace to control the extension of the elbow; the affected players used it regularly in practice and occasionally in games. Their elbow problem was controlled significantly.

What are orthotics and prosthetics? These two related sciences, while frequently linked together, involve separate specialties. Orthotics involves the use of bracing to correct and support a body part, while prosthetics concerns the utilization of artificial replacement limbs. Orthotists would be more likely to become involved with athletes. However, because a growing number of handicapped people are successfully participating in sports, it is not unusual for a prosthetic specialist to design a limb to enable an athlete to participate, for example, in gymnastics or football.

Although certified in both areas, Myers has concentrated his efforts in orthotics. Within this field, his subspecialties include pediatrics, sports medicine, and spinal deformities. For example, one device he has constructed to assist athletes is the body jacket (known in the profession as an anterior flexiform spinal orthosis). Myers has used the jacket to treat football linemen and gymnasts for fractured vertebrae. This injury is common to those types of athletes because of the stress and impact they put on their backs and spines. The body jacket has enabled these people to return to practice and competition.

Myers is typical of people who have recently entered the field. He graduated from the program of prosthetics and orthotics of New York University. Following placement in the field, working under the supervision of a certified professional for one year each in prosthetics and orthotics, he took his examinations to become certified. Satisfactory completion of these comprehensive tests qualifies a person as certified, and the designation CPO may be placed after the name, such as "Andrew M. Myers, B.S., CPO." Now the individual can engage in the profession. For information:

American Orthotic and Prosthetic Association
330 John Carlyle Street, Suite 200
Alexandria, VA 22314
www. aopanet.org

Sports Medicine Paraprofessionals

Love sports but don't wish to pursue extensive education? Consider a career as a paraprofessional. Numerous paraprofessionals assist in a variety of capacities in the sports medicine profession. The term *paraprofessional* here refers to health personnel who assist professionals (doctors and physical therapists, for example) in the performance of their duties. These aides, with advanced training and under supervision, recently have been permitted to undertake many of the duties previously handled only by professionals. Characteristics of paraprofessionals include:

1. Paraprofessionals serve under the supervision of a professional. The amount of responsibility given to the paraprofessional varies with experience and training. For example, a physical therapy assistant may provide rehabilitation instructions to an injured high school basketball player with a sprained ankle.

2. The career usually requires the completion of an education/ training program, normally at a community college. Some paraprofessionals may have shorter programs. For example, most podiatric assistants receive on-the-job training. However, to become certified, they must pass an examination prepared by the American Society of Podiatric Medical Assistants. On the other hand, physical therapy assistants are required in most states to complete a two-year college training program, followed by a state exam for licensing.

3. The nature of the paraprofessional's education/training resembles that of the profession to which it corresponds, except that it is shorter and more limited in content. For example, the physical therapy assistant program typically includes topics such as anatomy, physiology, psychology, physical therapy procedures, and philosophy of rehabilitation. However, it is not as detailed or lengthy as the course work required for certification as a physical therapist.

Paraprofessionals now work in many sports medicine fields. This offers the individual with an interest in sports medicine the opportunity for an enjoyable and rewarding career. Following are some examples of these occupations.

Medical Assistants and General Sports Medicine Aides

It is possible to attend college for two years and obtain an associate's degree as a medical assistant. The program at Arkansas Tech University focuses upon general knowledge combined with science courses and those related to office procedures and medicine.

Somewhat related are medical secretarial curricula. A number of business schools and community colleges around the country offer programs combining word processing or secretarial courses with courses on medical topics.

Many sports medicine professionals and clinics employ individuals as aides. These people, most of whom learn their duties on the job, assist both professionals and paraprofessionals. Many become very interested in their careers and seek schooling to improve themselves and their salaries.

If you are interested in the occupation, apply directly to the private offices of sports medicine professionals or to centers that specialize in sports medicine. Often these jobs provide excellent insight into the world of sports and make good summer positions. In addition, future job opportunities will continue to expand.

Sports Podiatric Assistants. Podiatric assistants help podiatrists perform functions related to the health of the athlete's feet. Among the assistant's duties are recording patient histories, preparing instruments and equipment, applying surgical dressing, preparing patients for treatment, assisting with routine office procedures, and similar tasks.

While many programs are developing to educate podiatric assistants, most receive on-the-job training. Many qualify for the Podiatric Assistant–Certified (PAC) designation from the American Society of Podiatric Medical Assistants. Eligibility for certification requires membership in the society and the passing of an exam prepared by it. Normally, certification carries with it improved prestige and increased salary. For information, contact:

American Society of Podiatric Medical Assistants
2124 South Austin Boulevard
Cicero, IL 60804
www.aspma.org

Physical Therapy Assistant and Aide. Two paraprofessionals aid the physical rehabilitation patient—the physical therapist assistant and the physical therapy aide. Physical therapy assistants graduate from a two-year program with a major in physical therapy, while physical therapy aides typically learn on the job. Both of these paraprofessionals work under the supervision of a professional physical therapist, who in turn works under the supervision of a physician. For information:

American Physical Therapy Association
1111 North Fairfax Street
Alexandria, VA 22314
www.apta.org

Other Sports Paraprofessionals. A variety of additional sports paraprofessional careers are available to those interested in sports medicine. The following organizations provide information for careers as dental assistants, technicians, and hygienists; orthotist-prosthetist assistants and technicians; and opthalmic-optometric assistants and technicians.

American Dental Assistants Association
35 East Wacker Drive, Suite 1730
Chicago, IL 60601
www.dentalassistant.org

American Dental Hygienists Association
444 North Michigan Avenue, Suite 3400
Chicago, IL 60611
www.adha.org

American Dental Association
211 East Chicago Avenue
Chicago, IL 60611
www.ada.org

National Association of Dental Laboratories
1530 Metropolitan Boulevard
Tallahassee, FL 32308
www.nadl.org

American Board for Certification in Orthotics and Prosthetics
330 John Carlyle Street, Suite 210
Alexandria, VA 22314
www.abcop.org

Joint Commission on Allied Health Personnel in
    Ophthalmology
2025 Woodlane Drive
St. Paul, MN 55125
www.jcahpo.org

American Optometric Association
243 North Lindbergh Boulevard
St. Louis, MO 63141
www.aoanet.org

You may also wish to consult the book *Opportunities in Para-
medical Careers* by Alex Kacen and Terence J. Sacks (VGM Career
Books).

CHAPTER EIGHT

Physical Educators

"Proposals Push More Time in Gym" Charlotte News Observer

"Fitness Report Cards Part of New 'PE' Movement" Education Week

"New 'PE' Finds Its Way into Schools" Houston Chronicle

"Kids Need School's Help to Get Healthy" USA Today

C hildhood obesity is now a national problem, proclaim the print and electronic media (and research study after research study supports them). The recent headlines above suggest that schools must deal with this problem, and teachers must be in the forefront.

Gym teachers, more properly called physical education (PE) specialists, have long occupied an important place in the hearts of youngsters. A background in PE can lead not only to jobs as physical education teachers, but also to many sports and health employment opportunities. Coaches often come from the ranks of physical education teachers, so this, too, looms as one of the attractions of the profession. Many states have regulations requiring each student in each grade to participate in a planned program of physical education. The program usually includes activities that:

- encourage each student to attain and maintain a desirable level of physical fitness
- develop competencies for lifetime participation in sports, team sports, and games
- promote an understanding of the relationship between regular physical activity and health

- provide sports, games, and other physical activities that promote self-confidence and the ability to work in a group
- require coeducation instruction at the elementary, middle or junior high, and high school levels

Current Trends in Physical Education

In recent years, there has developed an increasing desire to educate young people regarding the importance of fitness, the joy of sports and athletics, and the value of lifetime sports. The President's Council on Physical Fitness and Sports defines physical fitness as the "ability to last, to bear up, to withstand stress, and to persevere under difficult circumstances where an unfit person would be ineffective or would quit."

Part of this concern for youth fitness has stemmed from cross-cultural comparative studies in which American youth fall below their international counterparts. In addition, the desire to improve the nation's health has focused attention on school PE classes. For example, one Texas study found 39 percent of fourth graders, 37 percent of eighth graders, and 29 percent of eleventh graders are overweight. Further studies show that "an overweight twelve-year-old has only a 20 percent chance of being a normal-weight adult. By age eighteen, that chance drops to 5 percent."

Much as school curriculum changes in recent decades have occurred in other school subjects ("new" mathematics, "new" social studies), there has developed a "new fitness." It has taken several forms. Some of the most interesting have been the Play Factory at Emporia State University in Kansas and the New Games popular on the West Coast, which have emphasized the fun aspects of sports. Such programs have been based on concerns that people should have fun and that more people should participate in fitness activities, as opposed to focusing on winning or losing. This all represents a kind of throwback to traditional play—community play, children's games, social recreation—to the time when people played together as a way to grow closer. Some people who are not generally athletic or who have been inactive for years have been drawn to the new orientation. Physical education teachers have organized such activities at their schools with success. The leisure revolution has resulted in a desire to expand participation in lifetime sports. These new directions will continue to challenge and tax the energies and talents of physical education specialists.

In the last two decades, there has occurred a strong movement toward skill development in PE classes. Meshed with the new fitness, this can prove extremely beneficial in aiding young people. Gone are the days when PE instructors would throw out some balls and sit and watch the kids play or the class would play only softball because that's the sport the teacher enjoyed best. Quite obviously, many demands and duties characterize the activities of the physical education specialist. The following is a sampling:

- determines the ability level of students in their courses
- revises instruction based upon students' abilities; that is, in teaching a skill (throwing a ball), making it relative to what the class is able to do, and proceeding from that point
- prepares an equipment and materials purchase budget and maintains equipment once obtained
- utilizes an efficient system for reporting accidents and following them up
- conducts special programs for children with physiological and psychological problems
- provides information to the parents and community concerning the curriculum
- promotes physical fitness in the school and community
- helps students to commit themselves to self-improvement
- prompts nonparticipating learners to join class activities and stay involved
- develops a wide variety of skills in students, such as accuracy, agility, balance, coordination, flexibility, power, rhythm, strength, timing, and other psychomotor abilities

....

A Typical Day

The physical education instructor must maintain fitness, not only as a model for students, but also to keep the rigorous schedule that makes many demands upon the teacher. Consider a typical day in the life of a community/junior college PE instructor who served as a basketball coach. Frances Garmon, who has served at several schools, including Delta State College in Mississippi and Temple Junior College in Texas, has summarized a typical home-game day at the latter:

5:30 A.M.—Alarm clock rings: arise.

6:20 A.M.—Depart for college.

6:33 A.M.—Stop at store for three area newspapers; check the accuracy of game time and location.

6:45 A.M.—Arrive at gym and office.

6:50 A.M.—Check dressing room to see if everything is in order for the game—warm-ups, uniforms, shoes, socks, and training supplies.

7:00 A.M.—Call all local radio stations to remind them once again about the game. Make a short tape over the phone for radio broadcast. Leave any game-related information for the athletic office secretary.

7:45 A.M.—Review for class.

8:00 A.M.—Teach tennis class.

8:45 A.M.—Talk with and help students after class.

9:15 A.M.—Check to make sure the following people are prepared for the game: officials, clock operator, thirty-second clock operator, ticket takers, scorekeeper, announcer, concessions workers, and business office personnel. Also call to make arrangements to have game videotaped.

10:00 A.M.—Call the national office (NJCAA) and give them choices for top twenty rankings. Check mail. Call opponent to check if everything is okay and obtain arrival time of team.

11:00 A.M.—Teach swimming class.

12:00 P.M.—Lunch.

1:00 P.M.—Office work.

3:00 P.M.—Check out sound system, videotaping equipment, thirty-second and game clock, and all support personnel; have athletic secretary and cheerleaders call news media.

3:30 P.M.—Go home: change and shower for game.

4:35 P.M.—Return to gym.

4:40 P.M.—Double-check dressing rooms, gym lights. Go over game strategy.

5:30 P.M.—Meet with Temple team, discuss game plan.

6:00 P.M.—Greet visiting team; manager shows them to locker room. Talk with coach to see if everything is okay; may need location of a restaurant for postgame meal.

6:30 P.M.—Taping and individual talks with Temple team. Stretching exercises in locker room.

7:00 P.M.—Team takes floor for warm-ups. Coaches report starting lineups.

7:15 P.M.—Return to dressing room.

7:25 P.M.—Return to court; player introductions.

7:30 P.M.—Game begins.

9:00 P.M.—Game concludes. Talk with team in the dressing room and then with the news media.

9:30 P.M.—Check on dressing rooms; have managers and cheerleaders call news media not present at the game.

9:35 P.M.—Prepare statistics.

10:30 P.M.—Stop on way home for a snack.

11:15 P.M.—Prepare for following day's classes; prepare practice schedules.

1:00 A.M.—Bedtime.

For those individuals who mesh teaching and coaching, it's truly an unbelievable commitment. It requires intelligence, great energy, and solid ability, but it promises great rewards.

If you wonder why they do it, Pennsylvania teacher and coach Janet Lippincott offered an answer: "When these students begin to play on a school team, I know they already have a good background in technical vocabulary and body mechanics and can concentrate on perfecting skills and various strategies." By teaching students at both levels, she can see carryover of their learning, reassess the class curriculum depending on their needs, and, best of all, watch their growth and development.

Job opportunities have greatly improved for PE teachers; in addition, salaries presently are good and will continue to improve. Not yet convinced? Consider the following comments from Coach Bill Brosseau of Tolt High School in Carnation, Washington: "A window of opportunity exists to help young people, permitting a coach and physical education teacher to help a kid not only on the playing field but in life. I know this sounds trite, but it's true."

Following graduation from Salem College in West Virginia, Brosseau began coaching (football, track, lacrosse) and teaching (physical education) in New York State. A part-time job in a health club combined with a longtime interest in weight training and physical conditioning eventually led to a full-time position in sales and management in the fitness equipment field. However, he said, "I wanted to return to a school situation; one wonderful aspect of physical education teaching is these kids come to class excited and ready." At Tolt, Brosseau teaches two electives dealing with "strength conditioning and fitness development. I enjoy it greatly." In addition, he works on curriculum development, integrating physical education with academic subjects.

Education

Physical educators must obtain state certification as teachers. This takes place at a college that has an approved program for the education of teachers. In West Virginia University's program, for example, students take courses in four different areas: foundations, professional physical education teaching, activities, and a second teaching field and professional education. In addition to required courses, students may take electives in coaching, an academic area, or dance. Students examine a wide variety of practical and interesting topics in courses such as:

- Early Childhood Activities
- Movement Education and Rhythms
- Teaching Wrestling
- Teaching Volleyball
- Teaching Dance in Physical Education
- Curriculum in Physical Education
- Principles and Problems of Coaching
- Techniques of Coaching
- Water Safety Instructorships

The excellent program at the University of Wisconsin at La Crosse exemplifies basic course requirements, which include:

- Physiology of Exercise
- Human Motor Behavior
- Biomechanics
- Orientation to Exercise and Sports Science
- Safety, First Aid, and CPR
- Adventure Theory for Physical Educators
- Human Anatomy and Physiology
- Management and Instruction in Physical Education
- Evaluation in Health and Physical Education
- Teaching Health-Related Fitness

In all programs for teacher certification (teaching license), in addition to professional physical education subjects, courses must be undertaken in the arts, biological sciences, history and social sciences, and mathematics. Program requirements such as these attempt to provide the student with a well-rounded cultural education appropriate for a college graduate.

Student teaching is a special experience that is part of the certi-fication program. This activity finds college students, under the supervision of a cooperating teacher and college faculty member, instructing elementary, middle/junior high, or high school students. It is a period of intensive training. It is sometimes called an internship, residency, or practicum.

Most physical educators pursue graduate courses and master's degrees; a few earn doctorates. Some obtain graduate degrees in physical education, while others undertake work in other areas. Florida State University offers special courses of study leading to a master of science or doctor of philosophy degree in motor learn-ing and exercise physiology. The master's program has two areas of emphasis: exercise physiology and behavior with a track in motor learning/control. The doctoral program has subspecialties in anatomy, biomechanics, and exercise physiology. Florida State offers other programs in physical education at the master's and doctoral levels that are specifically designed for teachers or those interested in college teaching.

PE teachers obtain master's degrees for professional growth, financial reasons, and often to satisfy a state requirement. For a faculty position at a community college, an advanced degree is a necessity. For those wishing to obtain a position as a PE depart-ment chairperson or athletic director, advanced graduate work is required. Those seeking employment at the four-year college level will need to obtain a doctorate.

Getting Started

If physical education instruction may become your career, visit with a PE teacher and discuss your plans. He or she will be able to suggest a college as well as provide hints. In college, build into your program courses in communication arts, science, and busi-ness to permit greater flexibility upon graduation. While teaching may be your first choice, career opportunities expand daily in sports and athletics. It is strongly suggested that you obtain a student membership in your professional curriculum organization to help you stay current with your career and with potential job opportunities. Write to:

American Alliance for Health, Physical Education, Recreation
    and Dance
1900 Association Drive
Reston, VA 20191
www.aahperd.org

Canadian Association for Health, Physical Education,
    Recreation and Dance
403–2197 Riverside Drive, Suite 403
Ottawa, ON K1H 7X3
Canada
www.cahperd.ca

CHAPTER NINE

Additional Careers for Sports Nuts

This chapter briefly covers a variety of other careers related to sports and athletics. The jobs examined include equipment managers; statisticians; sports academicians; sports photographers; sports cartoonists; sports agents and representatives; sports museum workers; sports facilities architects, engineers, and drafting specialists; sports careers and the Internet; and sports organizations for women. Finally, this chapter offers an inside look at the world of professional wrestling.

Sports Announcers

Dan Baker has a unique position; he serves as the public address announcer for the Philadelphia Phillies baseball team and the Philadelphia Eagles football team. Dan's fine voice bellows throughout Lincoln Financial Field in the fall and Citizens Bank Park in the spring and summer. A veteran of many management positions in sports, he also serves as the coordinator of broadcast relations for Drexel University athletics in Philadelphia. As such, he assists in arranging radio and television coverage as well as on-air advertising for the Drexel teams, largely men's and women's basketball. Often he provides play-by-play or color commentary for broadcasts. Athletic teams need announcers—public address and broadcast; if you have a very good voice, this may be your opportunity for a fun career.

Equipment Managers

He has participated in the Mirage Bowl, Emerald Isle Classic, the Peach Bowl, and football games coast to coast. He is most proud of the "game ball" he received in a big win over Memphis State.

Who is this? Dick Hall, head equipment manager, U.S. Marine Academy at West Point.

Dick typifies those who love and wish to stay close to sports during their lives. He graduated from high school and found himself in the U.S. Army shortly thereafter. Following service in Vietnam, he obtained a position in the athletic equipment room at West Point. Soon he moved up to assistant manager and finally to head equipment manager. One of his many successes came during the Memphis State–Army football game. An unexpected drop in temperature prior to the game combined with snow made the artificial turf a skating pond! The team's regular shoes did not help. He took a chance and tried molded-sole shoes normally used on grass for a few players—they worked great. He quickly outfitted the team—the result: Army 49, Memphis State 7!

"As an equipment manager, you never know what kind of weather problems, what kind of equipment failure, or what kind of transportation problems you may encounter. You have to roll with the problems just like player or coach," believes Hall. "It's not boring and really makes for an enjoyable life when you love sports and athletic competition."

Sports equipment managers oversee the handling and care of everything from baseball bats to football helmets, largely at the college and professional levels. The equipment manager has the responsibility of keeping the team's equipment clean and in good repair, having the equipment available for practice and games (this means traveling with the team), and providing security for the equipment, which is the greatest problem of the equipment manager. Often the manager is aided at the professional level by an assistant and at the college level by student managers. Most equipment managers also perform other necessary tasks.

People employed in this profession normally have a great interest in the sport with which they are associated; often they have played or coached, and some have worked as salespersons of sports equipment. While no special training or education is necessary, a knowledge of the equipment and the ability to perform minor repairs are important. Also, the personal qualities of reliability and punctuality are a must.

Although equipment managers have been actively performing the craft for more than one hundred years, their professional organization has existed for only a few years. Presently salaries are attractive. Most equipment managers earn salaries from $18,000 to $50,000 annually, with the higher salaries coming at the professional level.

Bob Lambert served as equipment manager at Villanova University and also at the professional level. These jobs have kept him close to sports and allowed him to travel. "The job opportunities are great, and it's a wide-open area for women," Lambert said.

For further information, contact:

Athletic Equipment Managers Association
460 Hunt Hill Road
Freeville, NY 13068
www.aema1.com

Statisticians

Sports trivia buffs and rotisserie league fanatics can no longer claim exclusivity over sports statistics. Coaches have expanded their interest in this area, and the computer has emerged as a potent weapon in the arsenal. The data supplied by the computer add to the coach's knowledge of her or his team or the opponent; this information can assist with decision making. For example, the computer can process a great deal of data and find patterns. Football scouts can provide the computer with statistics on an opposing team, and then program it to provide information such as what play the team tends to run in a given situation. For example, the computer might predict that when losing in the fourth quarter, the opposing team tends to pass to the tight end on third down.

Statistics are kept at most levels of play. Which information is kept depends for the most part upon the philosophy of the coach. In basketball, one coach may want only rebounding statistics on the players; another may keep shot charts (locations of shots taken) and records of turnovers (the number and who committed them); and still others may keep vast amounts of other information on their teams and opponents. This may include such detailed information in a scouting report as the number of passes made between each player during a basketball game. Many high school and some college coaches record extra statistics, those over and above the minimal information kept by the official scorer.

High school and college coaches can be greatly aided by a competent student or volunteer statistician; likewise, the individual can gain valuable experience. Normally the coach has a prepared form on which to record the information. The coach explains the procedures to be followed and allows the aspiring statistician to gain some experience in intrasquad and preseason scrimmages. Once the season begins, the coach expects perfect accuracy. Interested individuals may wish to approach a local coach about aiding a team with statistics.

Experience will prove helpful. If you lack the background, you may wish to practice taking "stats" when watching a game or event on your own. While this is quite minimal, it might convince a coach of your desire to serve as a statistician. A knowledge of personal computers, data entry, and programming also will prove to be beneficial.

Careers as a sports statistician remain quite limited on a full-time basis; however, several opportunities do exist to follow this job as an avocation. It should be mentioned that developing some skill in this area will help in related areas, such as sports information and newspaper careers.

Perhaps someday you will emerge as the Sultan of Stat: as the director of the Elias Sport Bureau—the keeper of records for the National Football League and the National Baseball Association and a consultant to "ABC's Monday Night Football," *Sports Illustrated,* and many other organizations.

Sports Academicians

In addition to the professional programs offered by schools and departments on college campuses (physical education, sports medicine, sports administration, and other), academic departments often offer sports-related courses and research opportunities. Dr. Carl Morris, Harvard University professor of statistics and health care policy, spends a lot of his time analyzing baseball statistics—probably more time than most North Americans, even fans! Dr. Morris has a hobby. He has developed a system to analyze baseball so as to determine the value or contribution of every action. He typifies scholars who painstakingly examine an aspect of sports and athletics and then report on their findings.

Several scholars have begun to examine various aspects of sports from the perspective of their academic areas of study. These individuals have approached athletics and organized sports in systematic ways, armed with an excellent knowledge of how to conduct in-depth studies of a particular topic; examples follow.

- **Sports historians** examine such topics as the biographies of famous athletes and trends from past decades, such as the origin of a sport. They also work to encourage high school teachers to incorporate athletics into their courses when teaching U.S. history. Frequently, these individuals publish articles in the *Journal of Sports History* for the appreciation of the reader and the expansion of knowledge.

- **Sociologists** sometimes study the role of sports in society. For example, they investigate topics such as racial problems, attitudes toward winning and losing, the effect money has had upon athletes, socialization through school sports, and social stratification among athletes. Often they publish their findings in the *Sociology of Sport Journal*, the *International Review of Sport Sociology*, and other scholarly periodicals. Like other academics, most sociologists teach in colleges. Those with special interest in athletics frequently offer courses with titles such as Sociology of Sport or Sport in American Society.

- **Academic sports psychologists** examine such subjects as running therapy, mental toughness, and the psychology of coaching. These individuals have a particular interest in the mental aspects of athletics. Frequently, they provide guidance to players and coaches concerning how to achieve greater success through closer attention to the psychology of athletics. They work with coaches on topics such as motivation and the establishment of smooth working relationships among players; for the players, it means areas such as relaxation and pregame preparation. Articles by sports psychologists appear in psychological and professional coaching journals.

- **Philosophers** with an eye toward sports are involved in teaching courses and writing for the *Journal for the Philosophy of Sport*. They often deal with ethical issues.

Most jobs for sports academicians exist at the university level. This means that if you have an interest in this career, you will need to attend college at the undergraduate level and then continue through graduate school until you obtain a doctorate. A love of reading and scholarly activity is important as well as an ongoing desire to add to the body of knowledge of sports. Interested? Perhaps someday you may teach a course titled the Contribution of Athletics to American Culture or Management Techniques for Sports Facilities, or you might conduct research and publish a paper titled "The Mental Aspects of Pregame Preparation" or "The Value of Sports in a Small Town."

Sports Photographers

Want to be close to the action on the field or the court but have no penchant for coaching, officiating, or sports medicine? Then consider photographing or videotaping the event. Sports photographers capture on film some of the beauty of sports. A good sports photographer possesses excellent skills developed through many years of experience. If this sounds too demanding, consider beginning your career by "shooting" an amateur competition with a small camera or a rented video camera. If your interest grows, purchase equipment. Many local newspapers need photographs; ask them if they would like some of yours. You may even be paid! At the very least, you should receive a name credit with the photo. Many teams would greatly appreciate videos of their games for players and coaches to study. This may be an opportunity to gain some experience while aiding the team.

Jerry Gay, a successful, award-winning sports photographer, traced his love of his profession to his youth. In junior high school, he dreamed of someday becoming a big football star, but his dentist advised him to avoid all contact sports while he was wearing braces. So he became a photographer. He has said that becoming a successful photographer is like becoming a successful athlete in that it takes a lot of hard work and patience to make the major leagues—but when you get there, you're glad you paid your dues.

Some photographers work for specific magazines or newspapers. If these are general publications, the photography staff covers subjects other than sports; while a few photographers may specialize in athletics, they well may be called upon to work on other assignments. Naturally, those employed by sports magazines or newspapers would work only in athletics.

A significant number of photographers in this field work as freelancers. This means they are self-employed and contract to work for a number of publications. Some receive specific assignments to cover particular events and then sell the shots they take. Others work part-time for a couple of newspapers, supplying them with several photographs a week. Still others may attend games and hope they get some spectacular photos of an event to sell freelance to a magazine or newspaper.

Mike DiTrolio of Havertown, Pennsylvania, used his experience as a videographer to produce sports-related videotapes. He has produced football highlight films for Auburn, Maryland, and Rutgers Universities as well as for professional teams such as the Philadelphia Flyers. He has also made recruiting videos for many college sports teams. DiTrolio said, "The nicest thing about shooting sporting events is that it's exciting! I want to be ready to capture the great play—the touchdown in the end zone.

"There exists a significant difference between running my own business and working for someone else," DiTrolio pointed out. He previously worked for TelRa, a video firm headquartered in Wayne, Pennsylvania. "My business and interpersonal skills, in addition to my videos, need to be excellent."

Few opportunities exist for sports photographers; however, a small group do very well financially, combining excellent salaries with a glamorous life. You may wish to consider it simply an avocation (hobby) or an enjoyable second job. If you think you're interested, start now and take a photography, film, or video course.

For more information, review *Opportunities in Photography Careers* by Bervin M. Johnson (VGM Career Books) or write to:

Photographic Society of America
3000 United Founders Boulevard, Suite 103
Oklahoma City, OK 73112
www.psa-photo.org

Sports Cartoonists

He has captivated the sports fans of New York, who have avidly turned for years to the pages of the *New York Daily News* to follow his exploits. He is sports cartoonist extraordinaire Bill Gallo.

Bill Gallo captures in hand-drawn art the activities of New York players, teams, coaches, and owners—to the delight of his followers. In addition, he often also deals with national issues. Although Gallo has entertained the greater New York area for decades, few other papers or magazines have added a cartoonist's work to enrich the sports pages. Consequently few full-time positions exist for this specialized craft. Even Gallo writes on boxing as a columnist as part of his position at the *News*. His recent book, *Drawing a Crowd* (Jonathan David Publishers), has received rave reviews.

However, being a part-time sports cartoonist can serve as a profitable and lucrative hobby, and some magazines and papers have moved in the direction of hiring cartoonists. For example, Vic Harville has provided sketches for the *Arkansas Democrat* with his "Sportstuff" cartoons, Stephen Mellus has sketched "Draft Choices" for the *Middletown Record* in New York, and Steve Moore's "In the Bleachers" appears in the *Wilmington (Delaware) News Journal*. Many of these artists' cartoons appear in several newspapers. A slow growth should occur in this career, with most sports cartoonists obtaining part-time positions.

Sports Agents and Representatives

In this era of fantastic salaries for professional athletes, the agent has become a visible member of the sports scene. "Show me the money" has become a catchphrase related to this profession. Agents, also called representatives, act as the players' intermediaries with the team's owner and general manager to secure the best financial and playing arrangement for the athlete. The use of agents occurs in several professions; for example, writers use literary agents, and people in show business use booking agents.

Agents are usually lawyers or accountants. They obtain their salaries as a percentage of the income the client receives from the team (or athletic event, as in boxing). Agents normally receive 3 to 15 percent for their negotiation of the contract. When you consider the salaries of individuals such as Ken Griffey Jr., Alex Rodriguez, Lebron James, Donavan McNabb, and Michael Jordan, you realize that this sports career can provide excellent salaries.

Shelley Pennefather, former college All-American and basketball star for the Nippon Express team in Japan, said a good agent is critical to a player's success. "My agent, Bruce Levy, was particularly helpful in my continuing basketball following college," said Pennefather.

In addition to negotiating contracts, many representatives serve as financial agents for players, making suggestions for investments or product endorsements and handling income taxes. Some act as representatives for organizations, such as the football players' association, or for baseball's umpires. In doing so, they work to obtain better salaries, retirement benefits, and improved working conditions. A very good journal to read in this regard is the *Villanova Sports and Entertainment Law Forum,* which provides basic and sophisticated articles on sports law.

Sports Management Companies

Today, the trend is away from the single agent and toward the sports management company. For example, Pro Ex (Professional Excellence in Sports, Inc.) in San Diego, California, provides a full range of services for the professional athlete.

"The Pro Ex team of consultants allows us to offer the professional athlete an unmatched wealth of information to ensure the success of his career, both on and off the field," said founder David Morway. Services range from contract negotiations and estate planning to product endorsements and public speaking development.

ProServ, based in the Washington, D.C., area with additional offices around the world, has athletes under contract in a wide variety of sports. One of the nation's premier sports management firms, it has had excellent success in obtaining endorsements for its numerous clients, including Boomer Esiason, Michael Jordan, Greg LeMond, Brandy Johnson, Karch Kiraly, and Stefan Edberg. In addition, ProServ has organized events for companies to sponsor in the field of sports and athletics. In the fast lane of sports excitement and sports show business, only individuals with high energy levels and excellent negotiating and interpersonal skills should seek employment with a sports management company.

Many of the one-person firms have evolved into management companies for their individual clients. They may manage clients' moves and arrange product endorsements, earning a percentage of the profits in the process.

Agents for Nonathletes

Another important trend has been the movement for nonathletes associated with sports to seek agent representation. Presently professional and college athletic coaches, radio sports talk show hosts, television game analysts, umpires, and other sports-related people utilize agents to handle their contractual arrangements.

Richie Phillips is typical of agents representing these individuals. A well-known attorney, he has served as a representative for several players and coaches as well as the Major League Baseball Umpires Association and National Basketball Association Officials, playing an important role in negotiating contracts. Phillips said that "the representative lends objectivity to a situation, since the player or management may not be able to evaluate the athlete's contribution to the team, that is, the player's bargaining position." He has served his clients through careful examination of the language of contracts; for example, the wording of no-cut clauses. "If you're interested in the career, attend law school and do a good job for your clients," suggested Phillips.

For many years, players made their own arrangements with the team owners. With the introduction of television, rivalries between leagues, and the expansion of players' legal rights, salaries accelerated greatly. Many athletes in past years were underpaid for their performance; today some players are grossly overpaid. One can hope that a leveling of salaries will occur before sports are seriously damaged in terms of public support.

Opportunities for agents in the future will remain small (presently there are approximately twenty-five hundred agents in the United States and Canada), but the salaries will continue to be excellent. If you're interested, the best background is law and accounting meshed with outstanding communication skills, because if you can't convince an athlete to become your client, you can't get to first base!

The following book may prove beneficial to aspiring agents: *An Athlete's Guide to Agents* by Robert Ruxin (Stephen Greene Press). Also see www.sportsrecruitingscouts.com for more information.

Sports Museum Workers

Sports museums and halls of fame in North America stretch from Winnipeg (Aquatic Hall of Fame and Museum) and Toronto (Canada's Sports Hall of Fame) to Fort Lauderdale (International Swimming Hall of Fame) and Daphne, Alaska (American Sport Art Museum and Archives). They stretch from coast to coast, encompassing Cooperstown, New York (National Baseball Hall of Fame and Museum), and Springfield, Massachusetts (Naismith Memorial Basketball Hall of Fame), in the East through Canton, Ohio (Professional Football Hall of Fame), and Stillwater, Oklahoma (National Wrestling Hall of Fame), in the Heartland to Vancouver (British Columbia Sports Hall of Fame and Museum) and San Diego, California (San Diego Hall of Champions), in the West. *And they all—nearly a hundred facilities—need employees!*

Typical is the College Football Hall of Fame in Kings Island, Ohio. The facility houses several exhibitions, serves as a resource center for inquiries on the sport, and contains a library.

Most museums have film and video showings and other interesting activities. Most museum personnel fall into two categories:

the business group and the professional or creative staff. The businesspeople manage the financial aspects of the facility (budgeting, fund-raising, promotion, and advertising), while members of the creative staff design shows, assist visitors, direct library and reference services, and generally make the museum a fun and educational place for guests. The museum or hall of fame exists to honor a sport and translate the joy of it to others. The number of employees varies with the popularity and size of the museum.

For those interested in business positions, a regular college business program with a major in marketing or management would prove beneficial. Those with course work and/or special skills in fund-raising, public relations, and managing public (nonprofit) organizations will have an edge in garnering jobs.

Programs also exist for those on the museum's technical side. For example, Baylor University, the University of Southern California, and other schools offer programs in museum studies. Write to any college in which you are interested and ask about museum studies options.

The following organization may also prove helpful:

International Association of Sports Museums and Halls of
   Fame
180 North LaSalle Street, Suite 1822
Chicago, IL 60601
www.sportshalls.com

Sports Facilities Architects, Engineers, and Drafting Specialists

- The Skydome in Toronto
- Pilot Field in Buffalo
- The Camden Yards Stadium Complex in Baltimore
- The Florida Suncoast Dome in St. Petersburg
- U.S. Cellular Field in Chicago
- Citizens Bank Park in Philadelphia

These sports facilities are but a small sample of the recent sports projects constructed in North America. These structures, and numerous others on college campuses, provide wonderful opportunities for employment for people with special training in engineering, architecture, and drafting.

Growing fan attendance, the desire to upgrade older facilities, and continued expansion of professional franchises have resulted in a surge of new facilities and restructuring of existing ones. Individuals who combine a love of sports with specialized skills and knowledge will have the opportunity to personally have an impact on the games they admire. Architects, engineers, and often public relations specialists work on the initial design with the facility's owner. Speaking and interpersonal skills remain critical for these positions because often political leaders, voters, and others need explanations of the structure—and oftentimes of related costs and construction delays. Drafting specialists work as part of the design team under the supervision of architects and engineers.

A leading organization in the area of sports facilities design is Hellmuth, Obata, and Kassabaum (HOK). Located in Kansas City, this organization and its team of sports architects and related personnel (drafters, secretaries, and others) study "the feasibility, design, and development of sports and spectator facilities." The group's successes include Bradley Center (Milwaukee, Wisconsin), Memphis Downs Race Track (Memphis, Tennessee), Joe Robbie Stadium (Dade County, Florida), the Alamo Dome (San Antonio, Texas), University of Delaware Sports and Convocation Center (Newark, Delaware), U.S. Cellular Field (Chicago, Illinois), and Pilot Field (Buffalo, New York).

If this exciting field interests you, consider attending college and studying architecture or engineering. These careers require a demanding academic program. A quicker, but less lucrative, route might be studying drafting at a trade or technical school or community college. All of these individuals must not only have a great knowledge of their profession, but also an in-depth knowledge and love of sports. For example, Ron Labinski of the HOK Sports

Facilities Design Team on a visit to the Kansas City Chiefs' Arrowhead Stadium, where he served as project architect, noticed that the ceiling tiles had been removed above the taping tables. Upon further investigation, he found that the tiles had been taken out because many football players liked to stand on the athletic training tables for the taping of their ankles. Consequently, when involved with the development of Giants Stadium in the New Jersey Meadowlands, Labinski designed the ceilings two feet higher.

People planning on entering this career should integrate sports studies courses into their college programs whenever possible and maintain an ongoing interest in sports. In addition, they should gear course projects and field experiences toward sports facilities. The following organizations may be helpful to contact:

American Institute of Architects
1735 New York Avenue NW
Washington, DC 20006
www.aia.org

American Design Drafting Association
105 East Main Street
Newbern, TN 38059
www.adda.org

National Society of Professional Engineers
1420 King Street
Alexandria, VA 22314
www.nspe.org

Sports Careers, the Internet, and Searching

The growth of the Internet has expanded the horizons of available information about sports. This includes information related to employment possibilities as well as details of interest to practitioners in various fields.

For example, many professional organizations maintain websites through which you may access information. All you need to reach any such site is a computer with a modem and access to the Internet through a commercial online service or other service provider. By keying in a phrase such as "women in sports" or "Women's Sports Foundation," you can gain instant access to a wealth of information. The website for the Women's Sports Foundation includes the following details:

- background information about the organization including its goals, leadership, and members
- a description of four basic program areas: education (including a listing of publications and videotapes available through the Foundation); opportunities such as scholarships and grants; advocacy for change in policies, social patterns and laws affecting female sports and fitness participation; and programs honoring accomplishments of women in sports
- membership information and the organization's telephone numbers and mailing address

Information for coaches and other sports professionals can also be found on the Internet. For example, the *Journal of Basketball Studies* is an online magazine designed specifically for sharing information about effective coaching strategies.

Those seeking employment in sports-related areas can also use the Internet during the job search process. The Internet can be a great asset when it comes to looking for a job. Services such as America's Job Bank and other online job listings provide information about job openings around the country. You can browse through such listings and identify jobs of possible interest. Some listings allow you to search by job title or category. If you're interested in coaching, you might look under "education," "sports," or some related category. You can also limit searches to individual states, specific newspapers, or other characteristics.

Organizations for Women

Along with the growth in women's participation in sports, several organizations have focused their activities on women and sports. For example, the Women's Sports Foundation is a nonprofit organization that promotes the sports and fitness experience for women and girls. Established in 1974 by tennis great Billie Jean King and other female athletes, the Foundation provides scholarships, travel, and training grants for women and girls, paid internships related to sports careers, and other programs and services. Individuals are welcome to become members. For more information, contact the organization as follows:

Women's Sports Foundation
Eisenhower Park
East Meadow, NY 11554
www.womenssportsfoundation.org

Professional Wrestling Careers

One of the fastest-growing sports in North America in the last fifteen years has been professional wrestling. A far cry from what you see on the mats in high school, college, or the Olympics, professional wrestling has strayed from the confines of strict, uniform rules to become more of an entertainment exhibition than a sport. Also unlike the more traditional forms, professional wrestling includes women as well as men, although the sexes do not normally compete against one another. Professional wrestlers typically wear flashy costumes, with one combatant taking the role of the hero and the other playing the part of the villain. The audience boisterously cheers the hero and jeers the villain. The match takes place in a padded, roped-off arena similar to a boxing ring. The opponents may cling to the ropes or even jump out of the ring during the match. Tag team matches, in which pairs of wrestlers take turns battling one another, also are popular.

A variety of jobs exist in professional wrestling, from ring announcer and manager to promoter and television commentator. Naturally, most of the attention is focused upon the combatants in the "squared circle."

The explosion of cable television and syndication has brought the colorful and exciting spectacle of professional wrestling into the living rooms of North America. Its widespread popularity has made household names of Hulk Hogan, The Rock, Wendy Richter, Sycho Sid, Sambu, Sergeant Slaughter, The Road Warriors, Ric Flair, Jerry "The King" Lawler, and others.

Wrestling Lifestyles

How can someone enter this career? King Kaluha is an example of a part-time wrestler. He suggested, "It helps to have a wrestling or martial arts (like karate) background. In addition, athletic experience and weight training are a must." Kaluha, who has bench-pressed over four hundred pounds, has wrestled on the East Coast from Maine to Florida, usually in small facilities, arenas, and gymnasiums, on weekends or holidays.

King Kaluha said that wrestling is a great part-time job. During his first seven years of wrestling, he competed against some of the profession's most famous wrestlers—Tonga Kid, David Sanmartino, Rick Martel, Sergeant Slaughter, the Road Warriors, and others. He said, "I've always been an extrovert. The showmanship in this sport is perfect for me. There are not a lot of good wrestlers around. There are some big guys who can't wrestle or excite the crowd and some others close to retirement."

There are hundreds of professional wrestlers like Kaluha who work part-time. They may wrestle one to four days per week and lifts weights five or six days per week. People may pay them to appear at events such as birthdays or car sales.

"Nature Boy" Ric Flair offers the best in contemporary showmanship and wrestling skills. He has held the championship title in many organizations, including the National Wrestling Alliance (NWA), World Championship Wrestling (WCW), and the World Wrestling Federation (WWF). He wrestles in the United States, Canada, and other countries and has been one of the best-paid athletes in North America. He learned from a former wrestling champion, Verne Gagne, now retired. Millions have watched Flair's television performances, and from five hundred to twenty thousand people attend each of his live matches. Some weeks he travels only two miles, but other weeks he travels as far as Japan.

The life of a wrestler is very exciting, but it is also very hard work. Practicing takes a lot of time. Flair said, "I emphasize endurance training and weight training in my conditioning program. I even give my leisure time to athletic hobbies; I particularly like water sports.

"It's important to achieve athletically and academically," the world champion said. "The habits that you develop in school and college will help you compete in life and in the ring. In addition, read and study about topics that can enhance your athletic ability—for example, nutrition and weight training."

Not for Men Only

There exists a whole world of wrestling for women in the ring, not just as a manager, and it's growing. Typical is the career of championship wrestling pro Heide Lee Morgan, originally from Elmer, New Jersey. As a young girl, she pursued gymnastics as a hobby while also enjoying dance, basketball, and softball. She said, "Gymnastics gave me the excellent agility so important in successful professional wrestling."

In high school, she began weight training to shape and proportion her body. This resulted in her winning several bodybuilding championships, including becoming the two-time Greater Philadelphia Body Building Champion in the women's teenage division.

Having developed an impressive sports body, she gained part-time employment in posing expositions, some of which were at wrestling events. Finally, after the encouragement of numerous people, she attended the Fabulous Moolah Wrestling School in Columbia, South Carolina.

Her life in the wrestling world really began when she attended matches of her father. He wrestled as "The Crazy Yankee" and as "Little Abner." When he participated in the latter role, she would precede him into the arena dressed as the cartoon character "Daisy Mae" and give daisies to the fans.

Upon completion of wrestling school, Morgan started slowly with matches on the East Coast. As she achieved success and the fans began to take notice, she moved up to wrestle for the American Wrestling Association (AWA) and the prestigious National Wrestling Alliance (NWA). Her success included being a member of the Ladies Professional Wrestling Association (LPWA) tag team champions. Morgan's career has taken her to Japan, Italy, South America, Canada, and coast-to-coast in the United States. She stated, "One great fringe benefit is seeing the world and getting paid for it.

"Professional wrestling—as with life—causes you to make sacrifices if you want to be successful. However, one thing you should never sacrifice are your morals or values, or your reputation will be ruined," Morgan emphasized. She further added, "Women have been neglected and have not gotten their proper recognition in this business."

Getting Started

Professional wrestling today combines physical skills and showmanship. Therefore, future wrestlers need to develop good speaking skills.

Ric Flair and King Kaluha learned their profession as apprentices to other wrestlers. However, many future wrestlers will attend school to learn their skills. Wrestling schools teach young wrestlers special techniques of falling to prevent injury. The schools also teach different wrestling moves such as "body slamming," "suplexing," and "sunset flipping." There are many schools in the United States. Some of the well-known schools are listed at the end of this chapter.

"Opportunities exist for new wrestlers to rise to the top. But young people must remember that success requires developing a positive mental attitude and good habits," said Flair. His words apply not only to the game of wrestling, but also to the game of life.

Pro wrestling fans interested in training for positions as ring announcers, managers, promoters, and related careers should contact one of the wrestling schools. Prospective employees should remember that, as with other jobs, beginners should start small—in this case, with independent regional promotions—and after gaining skill and experience, graduate to the "big time" (the major wrestling organizations). Salaries for major professional wrestlers are excellent; those for most related positions lag considerably behind the combatants. However, if you love "show business and rassling," this could be for you.

For more information, write to one of the following wrestling schools:

Atlanta World Wrestling Alliance
4375 Commerce Drive
Atlanta, GA 30336
www.wwa4.com

Camp IWF
Independent Wrestling Federation
P.O. Box 110102
Nutley, NJ 07110
www.wrestlingiwf.com

Camp Martell
280 Kenilworth North
Hamilton, ON L8L 4R9
Canada

Combat Zone Wrestling School
1030 Route 47
Westville, NJ 08093
www.czwrestling.com

ECPW Wrestling School
87-A North Beverwyck Road
Lake Hiawatha, NJ 07034
www.ecpw1.com

Hammerlock School of Wrestling
P.O. Box 282
Ashford, Kent TN23 7ZZ
England
www.hammerlockwrestling.com

Hart Brothers School of Wrestling
International Championship Wrestling, Inc.
757 King Street East
Cambridge, ON N3H 3N8
Canada
www.allcanadianwrestling.com/hartbrothers/hart.html

"Killer" Kowalski's Pro Wrestling School
170 Pleasant Street
Malden, MA 02148
www.killerkowalskis.com

Monster Factory
(Pretty Boy Larry Sharpe)
P.O. Box 345
Westville, NJ 08093
www.monsterfactory.com

Slammers Wrestling Gym
P.O. Box 1602
Studio City, CA 91614
www.slammers.com

Women's Wrestling Academy
(All-Female Wrestling School)
The Great Western Forum
3900 West Manchester Boulevard
Inglewood, CA 90305

Also check www.wrestlingmuseum.com for information on the
history of professional wrestling.

About the Author

Ray Heitzmann has taught successfully in Pennsylvania, Illinois, and New York at the high school and college level. He served as a member of the adjunct faculty in the College of Allied Health Sciences at Thomas Jefferson University in Philadelphia. He received his Ph.D. from the University of Delaware. Currently he serves on the faculty of Villanova University.

A former successful athletic coach at the elementary, high school, and college level in New Jersey, Illinois, New York, and Pennsylvania, the author remains an avid student of the development and role of sports in society and performance enhancement of athletes. His coaching specialty features practice organization, strategy and techniques, and fundamentals development. Dr. Heitzmann has written several articles on sports and athletics; some have appeared in *Education Age, Coaching Clinic, Beachcomber, Philadelphia Inquirer, Illinois Libraries, Catholic Library World, Coach and Athlete, National Association of Basketball Coaches Bulletin, Career World, Philly Sport*, and others.

In the area of career education, he has authored articles for *Real World*, a career education newspaper for young people, and Career World, a career education magazine. His *Opportunities in Marine and Maritime Careers, Opportunities in Sports and Fitness Careers, Opportunities in Sports and Athletics Careers*, and *Opportunities in Sports Medicine Careers* were published by VGM Career Books.

Active in professional organizations, he has received the National Council for the Social Studies Outstanding Service Award, has been named Outstanding Alumnus by the School of

Education at the University of Delaware, and has received the MSCSS Gold Medal for outstanding research-based teaching publications.

Dr. Heitzmann speaks frequently at conferences, to high school and college groups, and on radio talk shows. The inventor of "Winner's Batter's Box," he has been fortunate to coach the following outstanding teams: St. Augustine's basketball team in Union City, New Jersey; International House, University of Chicago basketball team; Villanova University NiteCats basketball team (Little Seven Champions); Summer League Basketball Champions in Narberth, Pennsylvania; Sacred Heart CYO Basketball Champions in Havertown, Pennsylvania (Philadelphia–Mainline), New Orleans Bound (NOB); women's four-time championship flag football teams; and the many fine teams at North Chicago High School in Illinois, Highland Falls High School in New York, and Neumann College in Pennsylvania.